Living IN CHRIST

by Edwin Jiede

Revised 2004 by Clarence F. Berndt

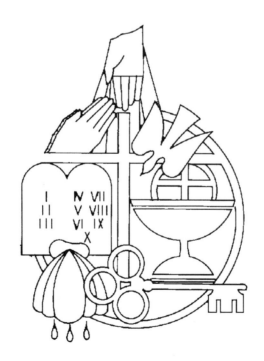

CONCORDIA PUBLISHING HOUSE · SAINT LOUIS

This book is the property of

_____
(your name)

_____
(your address)

_____.
(your city, state, and zip code)

I belong to_____.
(the name of your congregation)

I was baptized on _____ , _____

by Pastor _____

at _____.

My sponsors are _____

_____.

Written by Edwin Jiede

Edited by Clarence F. Berndt

Scripture quotations are taken from the HOLY BIBLE, NEW INTERNATIONAL VERSION®. NIV®. Copyright © 1973, 1978, 1984 by International Bible Society. Used by permission of Zondervan Publishing House. All rights reserved.

Hymn texts with the abbreviation *LW* are from *Lutheran Worship*, copyright © 1982 Concordia Publishing House.

Catechism quotations are from LUTHER'S SMALL CATECHISM WITH EXPLANATION, copyright © 1986, 1991 Concordia Publishing House.

This publication may be available in braille, in large print, or on cassette tape for the visually impaired. Please allow 8 to 12 weeks for delivery. Write to the Library for the Blind, 1333 S. Kirkwood Rd., St. Louis, MO 63122-7295; call 1-800-433-3954, ext. 1322; or e-mail to blind.library@lcms.org.

Manufactured in the United States of America

UNIT 1 The Existence of God
I Believe in God

I. To make true statements, write the words in the Word Box in the spaces below.

Word Box

loves
understand
holy
mind
merciful
alone
all-powerful
body
Friend
will be
known
unchangeable
will
was
forgives

1. Even the wisest men are not able to
   __ __ __ __ __ __ __ __ __ __ everything about God.

2. God hates sin in us because He Himself is __ __ __ __.

3. Because God is a spirit, He has no __ __ __ __ as we have,
   but He does have a __ __ __ __ and a __ __ __ __.

4. It is not possible to understand how God always __ __ __
   and always __ __ __ __   __ __.

5. With God nothing is impossible, for He is __ __ __ -
   __ __ __ __ __ __ __ __.

6. If we always remember that God is everywhere at the same time,
   we will never think that we are __ __ __ __ __.

7. Our great God remains the same; He is
   __ __ __ __ __ __ __ __ __ __ __ __ __.

8. Even our most secret thoughts are __ __ __ __ __ to God.

9. As believers we do not need to be afraid of God, for He is
   __ __ __ __ __ __ __ __. He is truly our dearest
   __ __ __ __ __ __. He __ __ __ __ __ us so much that
   He __ __ __ __ __ __ __ __ all our sins for Jesus' sake.

II. The Bible tells us that God has certain attributes. Write the number of each word in front of the Bible verse that teaches us about that attribute. You may have to use more than one number for some Bible verses.

We know that God is

1. everlasting   _____ The LORD your God is God; He is the faithful God keep-
                               ing His covenant of love (Deuteronomy 7:9).

2. good   _____ The LORD is slow to anger, abounding in love and forgiv-
                               ing sin and rebellion (Numbers 14:18).

3. invisible   _____ God is a spirit (John 4:24).

4. merciful   _____ "Lord, You know all things" (John 21:17).

5. omnipresent   _____ From everlasting to everlasting, You are God (Psalm 90:2).

6. forgiving   _____ The LORD is good to all (Psalm 145:9).

7. holy   _____ No one has ever seen God (John 1:18).

8. all-knowing   _____ "Do not I fill heaven and earth?" declares the LORD (Jeremiah 23:24).

9. unchangeable   _____ God is Love (1 John 4:8).

10. a spirit   _____ "I, the LORD your God, am holy" (Leviticus 19:2).

11. all-powerful   _____ "I the LORD do not change" (Malachi 3:6).

12. loving   _____ "With God all things are possible" (Matthew 19:26).

13. faithful

III. Fill in the missing words.

1. Others may not know whether I cheat, but I will remember that God __ __ __ __ __ all things.

2. I don't need to be afraid in the dark because I am never alone; God is __ __ __ __ __ __ __ __ __ __ __.

3. God knows every sin I commit, even when wicked __ __ __ __ __ __ __ __ come into my mind.

4. Whenever I sin, I offend God, my dearest __ __ __ __ __ __, who loves me.

5. When I find it hard to do my homework, I ask God to help me. He will help me in His own way because He is a __ __ __ __ __ __ God.

IV. Each of these Bible passages tells us some truth about God. As you read each passage in your Bible, choose a word from the list of 13 words in Exercise II and write the word after the Bible reference.

Psalm 138:1–4 _____

Psalm 136:1–3 _____

Psalm 97:12 _____

Psalm 36:10 _____

Genesis 17:1 _____

2 Timothy 2:13 _____

Jeremiah 10:10 _____

Psalm 102:27 _____

2 Corinthians 3:17 _____

John 1:18 _____

Psalm 139:7–10 _____

Psalm 103:3 _____

UNIT 2   The Triune God
In the Name of the Father
and of the Son
and of the Holy Spirit

I. Match the sentence endings in the second column with the sentence beginnings in the first column by writing the corresponding numbers on the lines.

1. People who have never learned to know the true God from the Bible

2. The only true God is

3. Father, Son, and Holy Spirit are

4. Although there are three persons, there is only

5. Because God is three holy persons in one divine Being, we call God the

_____ make false gods for themselves.

_____ Holy Trinity.

_____ three divine persons.

_____ the triune God, Father, Son, and Holy Spirit.

_____ one God.

II. Write T before the true statements and F before the false statements.

1. _____ There are three true Gods.

2. _____ The Bible tells us that there are three distinct persons in God.

3. _____ *Holy Trinity* means God the Father, God the Son, and God the Holy Spirit in one divine Being.

4. _____ God the Father is greater than either God the Son or God the Holy Spirit.

5. _____ People can understand how there can be *three* separate persons and yet only *one* God.

III. The three persons in God are mentioned many times in Lutheran church services. Look up these places in *Lutheran Worship*; check those that refer to the three persons in the Holy Trinity.

_____ The Invocation (p. 158)

_____ The Absolution (pp. 158–159)

_____ The Kyrie (p. 159)

_____ The Hymn of Praise (pp. 160–161)

_____ The Appointed Verse (pp. 164–165)

_____ The Responses before and after the Gospel (p. 165)

_____ The Apostles' Creed (p. 167)

_____ The Offertories (pp. 168–169)

_____ The Sanctus (Holy, Holy, Holy) (pp. 170–171)

_____ The Agnus Dei (p. 172)

_____ The Post-Communion Canticles (pp. 173–174)

_____ The Collects (p. 174)

_____ The Blessing (The Benediction) (p. 174)

IV. Each of these Bible passages refers to one special work that is ascribed to each person of the Holy Trinity. As you read each passage, write the text citation after the person in the Trinity that is described; then write the words that describe what that person of the Trinity does.

Galatians 5:22–23   Malachi 2:10 (first 2 sentences)   John 1:29

Father

_____

_____

_____

Son

_____

_____

_____

Holy Spirit

_____

_____

_____

V. Describe pictures (symbols) in your church that remind you of the triune God.

_____

_____

_____

VI. Many hymns mention the three persons in God. Find a hymn that mentions the Father, the Son, and the Holy Spirit. See _Lutheran Worship_ 168–175 for examples. Write an introduction to the hymn you select that would help your family or congregation focus on the message of the hymn.

_____

_____

_____

UNIT 3 The Bible
Your Word Is True

I. Cross out the word(s) that make the sentence false to create a true statement.

1. The actual words of the Bible are from—*men, God.*

2. *Some, All, A few, The important*—thoughts and words of the Bible are God's.

3. The Bible is the Word of—*God, men, Luther.*

4. There are—*few, many, no*—mistakes in the Bible.

5. The most important teaching of the Bible is to show us how we are—*to live, to behave, saved.*

6. The Bible is divided into—*six, two, three*—main parts.

7. The books of the Bible that were written before Jesus was born are—*Old, New*—Testament books. Those books that were written after His birth deal with—*Old, New*—Testament times.

8. God promises that when we read, hear, and believe His Word, we will be—*rich, blessed, famous.*

II. Check each true statement.

1. _____ All aspects of God's Word are true.

2. _____ The Holy Spirit gave men the exact words of the Bible to write.

3. _____ The Holy Spirit does not want the Bible translated into any more languages.

4. _____ The Bible teaches us the way to salvation.

5. _____ The Bible provides guides for living the Christian life.

III. Complete these special activities.

1. Write the names of the writers of the four Gospels.

_____   _____

_____   _____

2. Write O before the books of the Old Testament and N before those of the New Testament.

_____ Exodus	_____ Job	_____ Isaiah	_____ Colossians
_____ Psalms	_____ John	_____ Samuel	_____ Jude
_____ Timothy	_____ Mark	_____ Titus	_____ Luke
_____ Kings	_____ Peter	_____ Ruth	_____ Acts
_____ Genesis	_____ Jonah	_____ Daniel	_____ Matthew

3. Read each passage in your Bible. Underline the reference if it says that God's Word is true.

John 11:25   Luke 2:11   John 3:16   Revelation 16:7   Daniel 12:2

Numbers 23:19   Psalm 19:9   Psalm 91:2–4   Isaiah 25:1

IV. Listed below are some ways by which we can be blessed through hearing and keeping the Word of God. Examine yourself to see how you are doing in using God's Word for your spiritual growth by placing a check (√) in the proper column behind each statement.

	Usually	Sometimes	Never
1. I memorize Bible passages.			
2. I listen while the pastor explains God's Word.			
3. I study Bible history lessons carefully.			
4. I pay close attention while my teacher explains a Bible story.			
5. I participate in family devotions.			
6. I ask the teacher to explain Bible readings that are not clear to me.			
7. I try to remember something from Scripture when I am tempted to do wrong.			
8. I listen while the Bible is read in church.			
9. I read my Bible at home.			
10. In church I think of what I am saying and singing.			

UNIT 4 The First Commandment
God

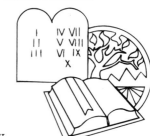

I. Read the Bible Teaching section of *Living in Christ* carefully. Then complete these sentences by using words from the Word Box.

Word Box

Word
Father
love
food
Son
His
money
Holy Spirit
trust
sum of all
First Commandment
hopes
God
all the others

1. The only God we should serve is the triune God, — — — — — — —, — — —, and — — — — — — — — — —.

2. Anyone who worships an idol breaks the — — — — — — — — — — — — — — — —.

3. It is not a sin to love our parents, but we sin against the First Commandment when we — — — — our parents more than — — — and — — — — — — —.

4. Some people make a god out of such things as — — — — or — — — — — —.

5. Any person or thing on which we set our — — — — —, or in which we put our — — — — —, is truly our god.

6. The First Commandment is the — — — — — — — — —.

7. The person who keeps the First Commandment will keep — — — — — — — — — — — —.

II. From the Bible Readings section of your *Living in Christ*, copy a Bible verse that would apply to each situation.

1. For centuries the people of one country believed that their emperor was a god and must be worshiped.

   _____

   _____

2. A father stopped going to church because he said God took away his little daughter through death.

   _____

   _____

3. A sick lady lost hope when her doctor said he could not help her.

   _____

   _____

9

III. Write the correct number in each space to show how each of the Bible people had faith and trusted in God. You can find all the answers in Hebrews 11:4–27.

1. Abraham   By faith _____ offered to God a better sacrifice than Cain did.

2. Noah   By faith _____, when God tested him, offered Isaac as a sacrifice.

3. Enoch   By faith _____ was taken from this life so that he did not experience death.

4. Abel   By faith _____ left Egypt, not fearing the king's anger.

5. Moses   By faith _____ built an ark to save his family.

IV. Circle the names of those children who showed love for God and trusted in Him.

1. Patty believed that carrying a rabbit's foot would bring her good luck.

2. Houa missed church last Sunday because he wanted to go fishing.

3. Lawanna joined her mother in listening to a Lutheran church service on the radio.

4. Cody attended church regularly during the school year because the teacher kept a weekly record. During vacation he didn't go to church.

5. Rob liked to memorize a Bible passage each day.

6. Claire prayed to God for protection during a storm filled with thunder and lightning.

7. Tabitha went to see a fortune-teller at the fair.

8. Glenn's mother gave him money for his church offering; he added some money from his allowance as an additional offering.

V. Write the answers to these questions. The Bible references will help you.

Psalm 64:2–10—Why does the psalmist think all people will rejoice in the LORD?

_____

_____

Proverbs 30:5—Explain the metaphor "God is a shield" to those who trust in Him.

_____

Proverbs 29:25—What is God's promise for those who put their trust in God?

_____

_____

Psalm 62:8—According to the psalmist, why is it good for us to trust in God?

_____

Proverbs 3:5—According to the psalmist, how much are we to trust God?

_____

_____

UNIT 5 The Second Commandment
God's Name

I. Match the sentence endings in the second column with the beginnings in the first column by writing the letter of the correct ending on each line.

1. God's name is used in vain when we _____

2. To use God's name in a joking way is _____

3. God's names _____

4. Swearing is sinful when it is done _____

5. Cursing means _____

A. wishing evil on ourselves and/or others.

B. tell us who God is and what He is like.

C. mock and despise God and His Word.

D. a sin against the Second Commandment.

E. falsely and carelessly.

II. Draw a line under the correct ending or endings.

1. It is proper to swear by God's name when

   a. a neighbor has been mean to me.

   b. it is done in court to tell nothing but the truth.

   c. we wish to appear important.

2. God's name is very holy, but it may be used when

   a. we wish to emphasize something we say.

   b. we really don't mean what we say.

   c. we sing a hymn or speak a prayer.

3. We have a right to call ourselves Christian only when we

   a. are members of a Christian church.

   b. make believe we are Christians.

   c. love Christ and lead a life pleasing to Him.

4. It is good to

   a. sing praises to God's name.

   b. laugh when people curse.

   c. say "Jesus Christ" whenever we are upset.

5. Using God's name in vain is

   a. a great sin, which God will punish.

   b. only a small sin.

   c. not as bad as it may seem.

III. Are the actions of these people right or wrong? Explain your answer.

1. Randy thinks he would be a sissy if he didn't say "damn" once in a while.

   _____

2. Eric won't play with some boys at the playground because he knows they use God's name in vain a lot.

   _____

3. Neil laughed when he saw a man bow his head to pray in a restaurant.

   _____

4. Juan asked a boy at school who used God's name in vain not to talk like that.

   _____

   _____

5. Bill says that as long as he himself doesn't curse, it's all right for him to play with boys who do.

   _____

6. Joanne loves to take her hymnbook and read the hymns that tell of Jesus.

   _____

7. Fernando says it's okay to say "for God's sake" if you don't really mean it.

   _____

8. Eric went to a fortune-teller.

   _____

9. Grandmother tried to cure Marti of her sickness by making strange motions and mumbling Bible verses.

   _____

   _____

IV. Read these Bible passages. Explain the proper use of or attitude toward God's name mentioned in the passage.

Psalm 34:3 _____

Psalm 142:2 _____

Micah 4:5_____

John 16:23–24 _____

Philippians 2:10 _____

Colossians 3:17 _____

Hebrews 13:15 _____

UNIT 6   The Third Commandment
God's Word

I. Place the words in the Word Box in the correct spaces.

1. In the Old Testament the Lord set aside the

   __ __ __ __ __ __ __ day of the week, Saturday, as His day.

Word Box

> worship
>
> Sabbath
>
> hear
>
> seventh
>
> every day
>
> rest
>
> Bible
>
> Christ
>
> Word of God
>
> work

2. The Old Testament Sabbath was a day of __ __ __ __.

3. The people of God kept the Sabbath day by not doing any

   __ __ __ __ and by hearing the __ __ __ __   __ __

   __ __ __ .

4. In New Testament times we do not need to keep the

   __ __ __ __ __ __ __ in the same way because

   __ __ __ __ __ __ has fulfilled it.

5. Sunday, Christmas, Easter, Pentecost, and other days are

   observed as holy days by Christians so that they will have time to

   __ __ __ __ God's Word.

6. Christians regularly __ __ __ __ __ __ __ in order to thank

   God for His gifts, hear His Word, and receive the Sacrament.

7. It is valuable for Christians to read the __ __ __ __ __ and

   pray __ __ __ __ __   __ __ __.

II. Write T before the true statements and F before the false statements.

1. _____ Normally we should attend church at least once a week, unless prevented by works of necessity and mercy.

2. _____ Christians chose Sunday as the holy day because Jesus rose on the first day of the week.

3. _____ It may be a sin to play soccer on Sunday morning.

4. _____ God wants us to study His Word and pray every day.

5. _____ To attend church "regularly" means "every time we possibly can."

6. _____ God commanded the people of the New Testament to keep Sunday as a day of worship.

7. _____ We sin when we miss church without a good reason.

8. _____ The Third Commandment requires confirmed people to receive Holy Communion often.

III. Underline the names of those children who have a good reason for not going to church.

1. Hal delivers papers early every Sunday morning and is too tired to attend by the time church begins.

2. Ralph and his dad like to fish on Sunday.

3. Angelique says she doesn't care to go to church because she can't understand the sermon anyway.

4. Joyce stayed at home because her mother thought she was getting the measles.

IV. Match the dates in the second column with the church festival in the first column. (See *Lutheran Worship*, pp. 8–9.)

_____ Pentecost (Whitsunday)   1. One week before Easter

_____ Ash Wednesday   2. January 6

_____ All Saints' Day   3. October 31

_____ Christmas Day   4. Friday before Easter

_____ Maundy Thursday   5. 46 days before Easter

_____ Reformation Day   6. 40 days after Easter

_____ The Epiphany of Our Lord   7. 50 days after Easter

_____ The Transfiguration of Our Lord 8. Thursday before Easter

_____ Palm Sunday/Sunday of the Passion 9. December 25

_____ Good Friday   10. November 1

_____ The Ascension of Our Lord   11. Sunday before Ash Wednesday

V. How would you answer people who give these excuses for not going to church?

1. I can read the Bible at home._____

_____

2. I know everything that is preached. _____

_____

3. Church lasts too long; I get tired of sitting. _____

_____

4. I need to get dinner ready. _____

_____

5. There are too many hypocrites in the church. _____

_____

6. Church is boring. _____

_____

7. Some extra sleep on Sunday mornings will do me more good. _____

_____

VI. The scrambled letters below give the names of people who listened to God's Word. Write the correct names of those people. The Bible references will help you.

DENIMUSCO (John 3:1–17)_____

USCHEZACA (Luke 19:1–10)_____

MONLOSO (1 Kings 3:5–15)_____

ELMUSA (1 Samuel 3:1–14)_____

UNIT 7 The Fourth Commandment
God's Representatives

I. Join the sentence endings in the second column with the correct beginnings in the first column by writing the letters in the spaces.

1. The Fourth Commandment tells us to honor _____

2. We sin against the Fourth Commandment when we _____

3. We owe our parents love and kindness even _____

4. Although the Fourth Commandment mentions only parents, it also means all others _____

5. We keep this commandment toward our government _____

6. When our parents send us to school, they _____

7. If our parents, teachers, or government officials tell us to do what is wrong, _____

8. Those who keep the Fourth Commandment faithfully are promised _____

A. disobey, despise, or hurt our parents.

B. a long and happy life.

C. by being helpful, law-abiding citizens.

D. our parents and others who have authority over us.

E. give the teacher the right to act in their place.

F. we must not obey.

G. when we have grown up.

H. whom God has placed over us at home, in school, or in the government.

II. Describe how each of these Bible people obeyed the Fourth Commandment. Look in your Bible if you do not remember.

Isaac (Genesis 22) _____

_____

David (1 Samuel 26:9) _____

_____

Joseph, as a boy (Genesis 37:13) _____

_____

Joseph, as a ruler (Genesis 46:29; 47:12) _____

_____

Jesus, as a boy (Luke 2:51) _____

_____

Jesus, as a man (John 19:26) _____

_____

III. Describe how each of the following people sinned against the Fourth Commandment.

The sons of Eli (1 Samuel 2:12) _____

_____

The boys of Bethel (2 Kings 2:23–24) _____

_____

Absalom (2 Samuel 15) _____

_____

The Prodigal Son (Luke 15:11–14) _____

_____

IV. Based on your knowledge of God's Law and His love for us, what comment might you make to each of these people?

1. Russ usually grumbles when his mother calls him from play to run an errand.

    _____

2. The boys across the street often laugh at their grandfather because of the way he walks and eats. _____

3. Jimmy quickly got up and offered his seat to an elderly woman who had just boarded the bus.

    _____

4. Gilberto and Hernando like to stay at home alone because they can do things their father and mother do not permit.

    _____

5. Florencia always takes a long time before she follows the teacher's directions.

    _____

6. Dameon wouldn't join the other boys in doing wrong because he remembered it would make his parents sad if they knew.

    _____

7. Jack tries different ways to make his teacher angry.

    _____

8. Hank spoke disrespectfully to the police officer who told him to wait for the green light before crossing the street.

    _____

V. Do you always realize how very much your parents do for you? Each Bible passage below contains a word that tells something your parents do for you. Read the passage and copy that word on the blank line.

a) 1 Thessalonians 5:17 (1st word)   They ___ ___ ___ ___ for me.

b) 1 John 4:7 (5th word)   They ___ ___ ___ ___ me.

c) Romans 12:20 (9th word)   They ___ ___ ___ ___ me.

d) Psalm 132:16 (3rd word)   They ___ ___ ___ ___ ___ ___ me.

e) Deuteronomy 6:7 (4th word)   They ___ ___ ___ ___ ___ me.

f) 1 Timothy 6:20 (9th word)   They ___ ___ ___ ___ for me.

UNIT 8 The Fifth Commandment
God's Gift of Life

Be kind to one another.

I. Complete the following sentences by writing in the correct words. Consult the Bible Teachings section of *Living in Christ* for help.

1. ___ ___ ___ ___ is a very precious gift of God.

2. God protects human life by His ___ ___ ___ ___ ___ Commandment.

3. The government has the right to take the life of any person who has committed ___ ___ ___ ___ ___ ___.

4. It is a sin against the Fifth Commandment to do or say anything by which our own or our neighbor's life may be ___ ___ ___ ___ ___, ___ ___ ___ ___ ___ ___ ___ ___ ___, ___ ___ ___ ___ ___ ___ ___ ___ ___ ___, or made ___ ___ ___ ___ ___ ___ ___.

5. In the sight of God hatred already is ___ ___ ___ ___ ___ ___.

6. God wants us to help and befriend our neighbor in ___ ___ ___ ___ ___ ___ ___ ___ ___ ___ ___ ___ ___ ___ ___ ___ ___.

II. Underline the correct ending or endings for these sentences.

1. When God tells us to love our neighbor, He means

   a. only the people living close to our home.

   b. only our close friends and relatives.

   c. only the people who have befriended us in the past.

   d. everyone who needs our love and help.

2. When our government puts a murderer to death, it is

   a. unchristian, because God wants us to love our enemies.

   b. unwise, because it will not bring the murdered person back to life.

   c. permissible, because God has given the government the right to punish law-breakers.

   d. unfair, because the condemned person cannot get a fair trial.

3. Hatred toward our neighbor should not be allowed to grow in our hearts because

   a. it could lead to actual murder.

   b. it makes us look gloomy.

   c. it makes us lose sleep.

   d. it is a sin against God.

4. If a person drives a car recklessly,

   a. she is ignoring the Fifth Commandment.

   b. the person is within his rights as long as he does not have an accident.

   c. she endangers the lives of others as well as her own.

II. How did the following people sin against the Fifth Commandment?

1. Howard was a poor swimmer, yet he often swam alone in deep water.

   _____

   _____

2. Julius pointed his loaded rifle at his friends just to scare them.

   _____

   _____

3. The airplane mechanic was careless when he inspected the plane.

   _____

4. Royce and TJ had a fight. Royce became so angry that he threw a stone at TJ.

   _____

5. Susan didn't like Joyce, so she told the other girls lies about her.

   _____

   _____

6. Tony had been told to stay in the house because his sister had scarlet fever, but he went out to play with his friends anyway.

   _____

IV. Check those things that the Fifth Commandment requires of us.

_____ controlling our temper   _____ attending church

_____ not quarreling   _____ befriending our neighbors

_____ obeying our parents   _____ making peace with our enemies

_____ worshiping the true God   _____ caring for our own body and health

_____ helping a sick neighbor   _____ taking care of a stranger who is hurt

V. Read each Bible passage and write a brief answer to each question.

Esther 2:5–7—How did Mordecai befriend his cousin, an orphan girl?

_____

What was the girl's name?

_____

Luke 7:2–10—Who showed love for a sick servant? How did he show that love?

_____

John 11:19—Who showed kindness to Mary and Martha? How did they show their kindness?

_____

Luke 10:30–35—In this parable who was kind? How did this person show kindness?

_____

UNIT 9   The Sixth Commandment
God's Gift of Marriage

I. Write words from the Word Box in the correct spaces. The Bible Teachings section will help you find the correct answers.

Word Box

- married
- union
- pure
- decent
- live
- work
- faithful
- prayer
- loving
- God
- unmarried
- clean
- God's Word
- spouse

1. Marriage is a lifelong __ __ __ __ __ between husband and wife, made by __ __ __ Himself.

2. When a man and a woman marry, they promise to be __ __ __ __ __ __ and __ __ __ __ __ __ __ __ to each other as long as they __ __ __ __.

3. The Sixth Commandment is meant for __ __ __ __ __ __ __ __ __ __ as well as for __ __ __ __ __ __ __ people.

4. A chaste and decent life means a life that is __ __ __ __ in heart, __ __ __ __ __ in speech, and __ __ __ __ __ __ in life.

5. Every married person should love and honor his or her __ __ __ __ __ __.

6. Our greatest helps in keeping pure are __ __ __ ' __   __ __ __ __,   __ __ __ __ __ __, and __ __ __ __.

II. From the Bible Readings in your *Living in Christ*, write the citation that teaches each of the following truths.

1. God joins people in marriage. _____

2. Husbands should be loving and faithful to their wives. _____

3. God wants us to be pure. _____

4. We should not hang out with wicked companions. _____

5. God has given us a prayer for a pure heart. _____

6. God wants marriages to last for a lifetime. _____

III. Write T before the statements that are true and F before those that are false.

1. _____ The Sixth Commandment requires me to be pure only when I am with others.

2. _____ A good way to defend myself from having unclean thoughts is to keep busy.

3. _____ One reason God wants my body to be pure is because my body is the temple of the Holy Spirit.

4. _____ It is all right to look at pictures of people doing indecent or suggestive things.

5. _____ In order to keep the Sixth Commandment, it is wise to run away from temptation.

6. _____ *Chaste* means "not married."

7. _____ I ought to choose only good companions, because evil companions may lead me to sin.

8. _____ Asking God for a clean heart helps keep our body pure.

IV. Think these questions over carefully, and write an answer based in God's Word for each one.

1. Describe three practices that help people resist temptations to do or say unclean things. _____

   _____

2. Explain how remembering your Baptism can help you resist temptation.

   _____

   _____

3. How can boys and girls protect themselves and others from unclean movies?

   _____

   _____

4. What are some ways of dealing with companions who want to do things that are displeasing to God? _____

   _____

5. Describe two things you can do to help your friends keep their thoughts, words, and deeds pleasing to God. _____

   _____

6. Which words of the Sunday service (in the Liturgy) are a prayer for clean thoughts? (See *Lutheran Worship*, p. 143.) _____

   _____

V. Look up these passages and then write the missing words in the sentences.

Proverbs 21:8—The conduct of the innocent is

_____.

Mark 10:11—A husband or wife who leaves his or her spouse for someone else commits

_____.

Hebrews 13:4—Marriage should be _____ by all.

1 Timothy 4:12—God's children should set an example for the believers in speech, in life, in love, in faith, and in _____.

UNIT 10 The Seventh Commandment
God's Gift of Possessions

I. Place a check mark (✓) before the actions that the Seventh Commandment forbids.

1. _____ cheating
2. _____ cursing
3. _____ stealing
4. _____ laziness

5. _____ borrowing
6. _____ gambling
7. _____ theft
8. _____ overcharging

9. _____ disobedience
10. _____ not paying bills
11. _____ false advertising
12. _____ not paying a fair salary

II. Place a check mark (✓) before those actions the Seventh Commandment supports.

1. _____ purity
2. _____ honesty
3. _____ giving to the needy
4. _____ giving to anyone who asks for money
5. _____ repaying what we borrow

6. _____ telling the truth
7. _____ attending church
8. _____ helping our neighbors to protect what they have
9. _____ being fair in business
10. _____ earning an honest living

III. Underline the best ending.

1. If you find money on the school playground, you should
   a. give it to your teacher so the owner can be found.
   b. keep it because "finders, keepers; losers, weepers."
   c. pick it up when nobody is looking and spend it later.
   d. put it into the church collection basket next Sunday.
2. If you tear a page in a book borrowed from a friend, you should
   a. return the book without saying anything.
   b. repair the tear and tell the owner when you return it.
   c. repair the tear and return the book without saying anything.
3. If an elderly person asks you to cut his or her grass, you should
   a. make certain you will be well paid before you take the job.
   b. refuse the job because you know you won't get paid much.
   c. mow the lawn because you want to help the person as God helped you.
4. If you see a reckless driver crash into a neighbor's car, you should
   a. keep quiet about it so that you don't get into trouble yourself.
   b. take the license number and tell the neighbor.
   c. say to yourself, "It serves him right."

IV. Underline the names of those people described below who are living according to the Seventh Commandment.

1. Chan accidentally trampled on some flowers in a neighbor's yard while looking for his soccer ball. He told the neighbor about it and offered to pay for the damage by cutting the grass.

2. Theresa often forgets to return pencils that she has borrowed.

3. When Alex returns from the store, he sometimes spends part of the change for ice cream without telling his mother.

4. Jerry is paid by the hour when he works after school. He works hard and keeps busy all the time.

5. Marti noticed a raggedly dressed beggar in the park. She encouraged her mother to help him.

6. Liu is small for her age and often rides the bus for half fare because the driver thinks she is younger than she really is.

7. Cory told the boys on Halloween night not to damage any property.

8. The boys, playing ball on the corner lot, broke a window in a neighbor's house. They all contributed some money to pay for it.

9. Mr. Smith has a large melon patch. Tony and his friends think it is all right to take a few because they won't be missed.

10. Kareem says it's not wrong to swipe things as long as you don't take money.

V. Match the sentence endings with the sentence beginnings by writing the appropriate capital letters on the lines.

1. In the Seventh Commandment God protects _____

2. The Seventh Commandment not only forbids stealing, but it also forbids _____

3. Sins against the Seventh Commandment start _____

4. We will gladly help our neighbor keep and increase his or her property when _____

5. We sin against this commandment when we are not willing to _____

A. every other kind of dishonesty.

B. the love of God dwells within us.

C. share what we have with people who need help.

D. our own and our neighbor's property and business.

E. in the selfish, loveless heart.

VI. In 1 Timothy 6:6–11 the Apostle Paul tells people to seek true riches. Study those verses carefully. Before each statement below write the verse number that agrees with the statement.

_____ Food and clothing are the most important bodily needs people have.

_____ A child of God, though lacking the luxuries of life, may be satisfied and happy.

_____ Craving for riches has led people to foolish and hurtful sins.

_____ At death we must leave our wealth behind.

_____ Coveting money may cause a person to lose his or her faith.

UNIT 11 The Eighth Commandment
God's Gift of a Good Reputation

I. Write the letter of each word on the line before its correct meaning.

1. ___ to give away our neighbor's secrets
2. ___ not true
3. ___ to tell lies about our neighbor and thus harm his or her good name
4. ___ to explain situations in our neighbor's favor whenever that is possible
5. ___ to tell lies to our neighbor or keep the truth from him or her
6. ___ bring, tell, spread news
7. ___ to shield our neighbor from harmful words or thoughts
8. ___ to speak evil of our neighbor in order to harm his or her reputation
9. ___ the quality of a person as seen by others
10. ___ cunningly; slyly; done with a will to harm our neighbor

A. reputation

B. mislead

C. false

D. betray

E. witness

F. slander

G. defame

H. defend

I. deceitfully

J. put best construction on

II. How did each of these people sin against the Eighth Commandment? Use your Bible to review the story. Write the letter in front of each name on the line of the sentence ending that completes the sentence correctly.

A. Gehazi (2 Kings 5:22, 25)

B. Judas (Matthew 26:14–16)

C. Men at Jesus' trial (Matthew 26:59–61)

D. Joseph's brothers (Genesis 37:31–35)

E. Ananias and Sapphira (Acts 5:1–11)

F. Potiphar's wife (Genesis 39:7–18)

G. Delilah (Judges 16:4–20)

___ Mislead people by their testimony

___ Misrepresented evidence

___ Lied about their contributions

___ Revealed an important secret

___ Lied to and about his master

___ Slandered a servant

___ Betrayed his master

III. Tell how these people obeyed the Eighth Commandment.

Jonathan (1 Samuel 19:4)

_____

_____

People of Capernaum (Luke 7:4–5)

_____

_____

IV. Explain what is wrong with each of the following statements.

1. It is all right to say harmful things about someone as long as they are true.

   _____

2. A lie is a sin only if it harms someone.

   _____

   _____

3. If most people believe a person has done a certain sin, I may as well agree with them; even though I haven't heard the whole story, the majority is usually right.

   _____

   _____

4. You cannot harm someone's body by saying evil things about that person.

   _____

   _____

5. I'm to blame for starting a bad story about someone, but it's not my fault if other people spread it and make it worse._____

   _____

6. If my friend has done wrong, I should try to cover up his fault by saying he did not do it.

   _____

   _____

   _____

7. It isn't a sin if we tell a lie in court in order to get a friend out of trouble.

   _____

   _____

V. Rate your behavior in these areas by checking (✓) the proper column

	Usually	Seldom	Never
1. When the children say mean things about a playmate behind his back, I take his side.			
2. When I hear something bad about someone, I don't tell others.			
3. When I am told a secret, I am careful not to give it away.			
4. If the ticket seller at the theater asks my age, I tell the truth.			
5. When I have done wrong, I admit it when my teacher asks me.			
6. If I have made trouble for someone by lying about her, I go to the person, admit my lie, and ask for forgiveness.			
7. I keep careful watch on my tongue so I do not say mean things about anyone.			
8. I try to say good things about people.			
9. I try hard not to lie even about little things.			

UNIT 12 The Ninth and Tenth Commandments
God's Gift of Contentment

I. Write the words in the Word Box in the correct spaces.

Word Box

satisfied
sinful
holy
one
covet
heart
envy

1. The ___ ___ ___ important lesson taught in the last two commandments is that we should not ___ ___ ___ ___ our neighbor because of the things he or she owns, nor try to get them by ___ ___ ___ ___ ___ ___ means.

2. To sinfully wish for things that belong to someone else is to ___ ___ ___ ___ ___.

3. Lying, stealing, adultery, and even murder are evil deeds that have their beginning in a covetous ___ ___ ___ ___ ___.

4. God wants our hearts to be filled with ___ ___ ___ ___ desires only, and He wants us to be ___ ___ ___ ___ ___ ___ ___ ___ ___ with what we have.

II. Write each of the words in the Word Box in front of its definition.

Word Box

covet
house
force
scheme
appears right
urge
inheritance
estrange
entice

1. ___ ___ ___ ___ ___ ___ ___ ___ ___ ___ ___ — items that a person receives when his or her parents die

2. ___ ___ ___ ___ —encourage; ask to do

3. ___ ___ ___ ___ ___ ___ ___ ___ ___ —cause to act strange; make a stranger to

4. ___ ___ ___ ___ ___ — sinfully wish for things that belong to others

5. ___ ___ ___ ___ ___ ___ ___ ___   ___ ___ ___ ___ ___ — tries to make a sin seem okay

6. ___ ___ ___ ___ ___ ___ — a sly plot to get what you want

7. ___ ___ ___ ___ ___ ___ —coax

8. ___ ___ ___ ___ ___ —anything that belongs to our neighbor

9. ___ ___ ___ ___ ___ —make someone obey you

III. Tell whether or not these people obeyed the last two commandments. Give a reason for your answer.

1. Mariah would like to wear fine clothes as some of her girlfriends do, but her parents can't afford them. She doesn't complain or grumble.

_____

2. Jess can't play basketball well enough to make the school team. This hurts his pride, so he no longer talks with the boys who did make the team.

_____

3. Lo Chen is a fast runner, but she lost the race at the picnic. She said some nasty things to the winner to make her feel bad.

_____

4. Sam had his leg crushed in a car accident. Even though he wishes that he could play with the other boys, he doesn't complain.

_____

IV. It is not a sin to wish for various things. When people continue to covet things they know they cannot have, however, they sometimes drive themselves to commit great sins. Such was the case with Ahab. Explain how each of these people was driven to sin by coveting.

1. Shantelle cheated on her math test and got the highest grade in her class.

_____

2. Shawn saw a ball game for half price by telling the gatekeeper he was younger than he really was.

_____

3. In order to fit in, Joni took a fine bottle of perfume when the clerk was not looking.

_____

4. Susanne kept part of her church offering money so she could buy candy.

_____

5. Dick hit the boy who beat him in the chess tournament.

_____

V. Read these passages in your Bible and write brief answers to each question.

Galatians 5:26—Since we live by the Spirit, what activities should we avoid?

_____

Proverbs 30:8–9—What is a God-pleasing attitude toward poverty and riches?

_____

_____

1 Timothy 6:8—With what did the apostle Paul urge Timothy to be content?

_____

1 Timothy 6:10—What is the root of all evil?

_____

Matthew 6:33—What is the most important thing a Christian should seek?

_____

UNIT 13 The Close
of the Commandments
The Judgments and Promises of God

I. Write the Bible verses that show these statements are false.

1. The worst punishment that can come from disobeying the commandments is the punishment we get from our parents or the government.

   _____

   _____

2. Not much good comes from trying to keep the commandments since we cannot earn heaven by doing good works.

   _____

   _____

3. Since God loves us as a father loves his children, He does not mind it when we sin.

   _____

II. Draw a line under the correct ending for each sentence.

1. *God is jealous* means that He
   a. is holy.
   b. insists on strict and perfect obedience.
   c. does not want us to worship other gods.

2. *Punishing the children for the sin of the fathers* means that God
   a. sends us His Holy Spirit.
   b. will forgive sins.
   c. punishes sins.

3. *Punishing the children for the sin of the fathers* means that God
   a. punishes children who follow in their parents' sins.
   b. hates children whose parents have sinned greatly.
   c. punishes children who disobey their parents.

III. Write T before the true statements and F before those that are false.

1. _____ God has a right to tell us what to do and what not to do because He made us; we are His children.

2. _____ God does not expect us to keep *all* the commandments because He knows we cannot possibly obey them perfectly.

3. _____ People who hate and disobey God make Him angry and bring upon themselves eternal death in hell.

4. _____ We should fear the anger of God.

5. _____ God only blesses believers who keep His commandments as best they can.

6. _____ God promises a reward so that we will *want* to love and trust in Him and gladly keep His commandments.

IV. Circle the R if God chose to bless the person(s) and circle the P if God chose to punish the person(s).

R	P	Pharaoh (Exodus 14:23–28)
R	P	Judas (Matthew 27:1–5)
R	P	Abel (Genesis 4:4)
R	P	Absalom (2 Samuel 18:9–15)
R	P	Saul (1 Samuel 31:1–6)
R	P	people of Noah's time (Genesis 7:17–24)
R	P	Mary, the mother of Jesus (Luke 1:26–38)
R	P	King Ahab (1 Kings 21:1–16)
R	P	Joseph (Genesis 41:38–44)
R	P	Cain (Genesis 4:5–16)
R	P	Ruth (Ruth 2:10–13)
R	P	Elijah (2 Kings 2:9–11)
R	P	Goliath (1 Samuel 17:41–50)
R	P	Abraham (Genesis 22:15–18)
R	P	Adam and Eve (Genesis 3:16–24)
R	P	Simeon (Luke 2:25–32)
R	P	Daniel (Daniel 6:23)

VI. In a paragraph describe the blessings God gives to those who keep His commandments.

_____

_____

_____

UNIT 14 The Purposes and Fulfillment of God's Law
"Follow Me"

I. Use the Bible Teachings section to help you complete these sentences.

1. Another name for the commandments is the ___ ___ ___.

2. The Law is holy and good because it ___ ___ ___ ___ ___ ___ ___ ___ ___ ___ ___ ___.

3. The Law cannot make us ___ ___ ___ ___ or ___ ___ ___ ___ us to ___ ___ ___ ___ ___ ___.

4. No person loves God with all his or her heart; therefore no one can obey the commandments as God ___ ___ ___ ___ ___ us to ___ ___ ___ ___ them.

5. The Law shows us that we are ___ ___ ___ ___ and ___ ___ ___ ___ ___ ___ ___ ___ ___; we cannot ___ ___ ___ ___ ourselves.

6. God sent Christ Jesus to keep the Law for us, and thus we have been ___ ___ ___ ___ ___ ___ ___ ___ by our Savior ___ ___ ___ ___ ___ ___ ___ ___ ___ ___ ___.

II. The following sentences state incorrect ideas. Cross out the incorrect words and complete each sentence correctly.

1. The Law was first written by Moses. _____

_____

2. God intended the Law only for the Jewish people. _____

_____

3. God gave the Law to frighten people into loving Him. _____

_____

4. God took Elijah into heaven alive because he kept the Law perfectly. _____

_____

5. Some people hardly ever sin. _____

_____

6. Jesus' mother, Mary, did not sin. _____

_____

7. There is no sin in a baby who is a day old. _____

_____

8. The reason all people sin is that they do not try hard enough to keep the Law. _____

_____

9. Children do not need the Savior as much as grown people do because children have not committed as many sins as adults have. _____

_____

10. God punishes only the sins people commit on purpose. _____

_____

11. We do not need to confess our sins until we are old enough to attend Holy Communion. _____

III. Look up each of the following verses in your Bible. Match each one with the truth it teaches by writing the number in the correct space.

1 John 3:4 _____   1. Without the Law I would not know which acts are sinful.

Genesis 8:21 _____   2. God's Word (the Law) lights my path so I do not go astray.

Psalm 51:5 _____   3. Every time I transgress (break) God's Law, I sin.

Romans 7:7 _____   4. The devil is controlling us when we sin.

Romans 5:12 _____   5. Adam (and Eve) brought sin into the world.

Romans 6:23 _____   6. I was sinful the moment I was born.

Psalm 119:105 ____   7. Children have evil thoughts in their hearts.

Romans 10:4 _____   8. Death comes from sin.

1 John 3:8 _____   9. Jesus saved me from the curse of sin.

IV. Put a check mark (✓) before the activities that help boys and girls resist sin.

1. _____ going to movies that contain filthy language

2. _____ praying for a holy heart

3. _____ looking at pictures that show people in very revealing clothing

4. _____ using God's name to curse people

5. _____ participating in church services

6. _____ memorizing the commandments

7. _____ cheating to complete school lessons

8. _____ continuing to play with boys and girls who start fights

9. _____ gladly hearing and learning God's Word

V. Complete one of the following projects on a separate sheet of paper.

1. Write a prayer in which you ask God graciously to help you keep from committing a sin you often do.

2. Write a letter to a friend explaining why he or she needs the Savior.

3. Write the names of three sins commonly done by children; then explain what children, with God's help, might do to resist committing these sins.

UNIT 15 The First Article—Creation
God the Creator

"The earth is the LORD's and everything in it." (Psalm 24:1)

I. Place the number of each term on the line in front of its explanation.

1. in the beginning
2. made by the power of God's Word
3. can be seen with our eyes
4. what the Apostles believed
5. cannot be seen
6. creed
7. is able to do whatever He pleases
8. creator

_____ Apostles' Creed

_____ maker

_____ statement of what a person believes

_____ before time was begun by God

_____ almighty

_____ visible

_____ created

_____ invisible

II. To make true sentences, join the sentence beginnings in Group One with the correct endings from Group Two by writing the numbers on the lines.

GROUP ONE

A. By His almighty Word God _____

B. God Almighty is _____

C. Because I know that God can do anything, I _____

D. God wants me to trust in Him _____

E. When we say the Apostles' Creed, we tell others _____

GROUP TWO

1. look to Him for help in every need.

2. to work out everything in my life for my eternal good.

3. made all things out of nothing.

4. what we believe about the God who made us and saved us.

5. my loving Father through Christ.

III. Use *Lutheran Worship* to answer these questions.

1. When do churches use creeds in their worship services (p. 185)?

_____

_____

2. Which creed do we confess when we celebrate Holy Communion?

_____

_____

3. Which doctrine does the Nicene Creed explain more fully than does the Apostles' Creed?

_____

_____

IV. All things God created were intended for the good of all people. List five things for which you are especially thankful to God.

1. _____

2. _____

3. _____

4. _____

5. _____

V. All of God's creation shows His great wisdom. Explain how each of these creations shows God's wisdom.

1. acorn _____

2. bat _____

3. snowflake _____

4. the seasons _____

5. stars _____

6. cactus _____

VI. Study the following passages in your Bible: Malachi 2:10; Revelation 4:11; Psalm 95:6; Hebrews 3:4; Psalm 40:4. Then write your own creed in which you state what you believe about God the Father.

_____

_____

_____

_____

_____

_____

_____

_____

_____

_____

UNIT 16 The First Article—Creation
Angels

"Praise Him, all His angels." (Psalm 148:2)

I. Write the Bible passages that express each of these truths. Consult the Bible Readings section of *Living in Christ* for help.

1. All the holy angels will be with Jesus when He comes on the Last Day.

   _____

   _____

2. Angels have no flesh and blood.

   _____

   _____

3. God sends good angels to serve believers.

   _____

   _____

4. Good angels protect us from harm.

   _____

   _____

5. Evil angels are angels who were thrown out of heaven because they sinned.

   _____

   _____

II. If a term below is true of good angels, write a G before it. If a term is true of bad angels, write a B before it. Some of the terms are true of both good and bad angels.

_____ invisible	_____ want to destroy people	_____ praise God
_____ created holy	_____ holy	_____ protect people
_____ sinful	_____ disobeyed God	_____ serve God
_____ hate God	_____ great number	_____ never die
_____ rejected by God	_____ great power	_____ spirits

III. Underline the names of those boys and girls who understand and make use of the truths about God's angels.

1. Alicia believes that her grandma became an angel when she died.

2. Harv does not believe that he has a guardian angel because he has never seen one.

3. Bruce rides his bicycle carelessly because he counts on the protection of his guardian angel.

4. Christine believes that one angel is stronger than a whole army.

5. Dominique has never been hit by a car, although he has crossed a busy street to and from school for five years. He regularly thanks God for sending angels to protect him.

6. Kaylynn prays to her guardian angel every night.

7. Nicky asks God every morning to send His guardian angel to be with her that day.

IV. Answer these questions.

1. Why are angels seldom seen? _____

_____

2. At times God gave angels special bodies so they could be seen. Our lesson gives one such story. What other Bible stories include angels that were seen?

_____

3. What other duties do God's angels have beside serving His children? _____

_____

4. What are some ways by which we can be safe from the temptations of evil angels?

_____

5. Why did angels help Jesus in the Garden of Gethsemane?

_____

V. The Bible mentions many occasions when God's holy angels carried out His will. Read each passage; then describe what God sent an angel to do in each instance.

2 Kings 19:35 _____

_____

Daniel 6:18–22 _____

_____

Matthew 2:13 _____

_____

Luke 2:8–14 _____

_____

Luke 24:1–7 _____

_____

Acts 1:9–11 _____

_____

Acts 12:5–10 _____

_____

UNIT 17 The First Article—Creation
God Creates People

"From one man He made every nation." (Acts 17:26)

I. Describe four ways in which people differ from animals.

1. _____
2. _____
3. _____
4. _____

II. Underline the words or phrases that describe Adam and Eve in Paradise before the fall into sin.

holy

possessed a soul that will never die

afraid of God

perfectly happy

sinful

possessed a body that will never die

loved God with all their heart

perfectly healthy

knew pain and sorrow

perfectly obedient to God

III. David said, "I am wonderfully made" (Psalm 139:14). Choose a part of your body. Describe how this part of your body is a wonderful blessing to you.

_____
_____
_____
_____
_____
_____
_____

✠ [LORD,] I praise You because I am fearfully and wonderfully made. ✠ Psalm 139:14

IV. Write Yes if the statement reflects the teaching of God's Word; write No if it does not reflect the teaching of God's Word.

1. _____ Our body is more wonderful than the finest machine that has ever been made.

2. _____ After death our body returns to the dust of the earth.

3. _____ God created human life; human life did not evolve from other life forms.

4. _____ Adam and Eve were exactly like angels when God made them.

5. _____ God formed Eve from the dust of the ground.

V. Word Puzzle

Unscramble each Clue Word and write its letters in the box on the right. Then, to state a biblical truth for your life, copy the letters in the numbered boxes into the boxes below that have the same numbers.

Creation

Clue Word

GSSEINE

SEODUX

UITICLVSE

SEUMBRN

RYDNUOETMEO

HUTTAECENP

NEOTARCI

ALLF

PORISME

UNIT 18 The First Article—Creation
God, the Preserver

"I will fear no evil, for You are with me." (Psalm 23:4)

I. Number these thoughts in the order in which they are found in Luther's explanation of the First Article.

_____ God defends me against danger and evil.

_____ For God's love given to me, I thank, serve, and obey Him.

_____ God made me and everything that exists.

_____ I do not deserve God's goodness. He provides for me because He loves me.

_____ God gives us all that we need to support our lives.

II. Write the words in the Word Box in the correct spaces.

Word Box

shelter
serve
praise
good
deserve
Father
danger
clothing
life
preserves
food
evil

1. God gives ___ ___ ___ ___ and also ___ ___ ___ ___ ___ ___ ___ ___ ___ it.

2. God preserves our life by giving us ___ ___ ___ ___ ___ ___ ___ ___, ___ ___ ___ ___, and ___ ___ ___ ___ ___ ___ ___, and also by defending us from ___ ___ ___ ___ ___ ___ and shielding us from ___ ___ ___ ___.

3. Even the evil that God allows to come to believers at times is really for their ___ ___ ___ ___.

4. God cares for us as our loving ___ ___ ___ ___ ___ ___, even though we do not ___ ___ ___ ___ ___ ___ ___ His goodness.

5. God's great goodness should lead us to ___ ___ ___ ___ ___ ___ Him and gladly ___ ___ ___ ___ ___ Him.

III. Draw a line under the word(s) in parentheses that make(s) the statement correct.

1. God supports the life of *(believers—unbelievers—every living thing)*.

2. God gives us *(all—some—most)* things that we need to support our life.

3. When God lets evil come to believers, it is for *(punishment—their good)*.

4. God's loving care is something we *(do not deserve—have partly earned—can demand of Him)*.

5. We should gladly serve God because *(He will punish our disobedience—He is very good to us—He will reward us)*.

IV. Underline the names of the children who are showing that they are thankful for God's loving preservation.

1. Will narrowly escaped being hit by a car. He remembered that night to thank God.

2. Li Soo doesn't think about what she's saying when she prays after meals.

3. The first night Paul was in the hospital after his bicycle accident, he didn't want to say the first part of Luther's Evening Prayer.

4. Helene is healthy and happy, but she usually doesn't pay attention when God's Word is taught in her class.

5. Shammah was deathly sick with scarlet fever. Every day she said a special prayer of thanks. When she finally recovered, she knelt beside her bed, folded her hands, and gave thanks to God for her healthy body.

6. Nicole's parents aren't rich, but they love their Savior and have led her to know Him. She thanks God for having given her such parents.

7. Bret usually misses church on Thanksgiving Day because he likes to watch the football game.

V. Look up these passages in your Bible and then write the missing words.

Matthew 10:29—Our heavenly Father cares even for _____.

Matthew 10:30—God watches over our whole body; God knows even the number of _____ we have.

Psalm 103:13—Just as a father loves his children, so the LORD loves

_____ _____ _____

_____.

Psalm 121:7—God keeps us from all _____. He watches over our

_____.

Psalm 136:25—God gives food to all _____.

Matthew 6:28–30—God clothes the lilies of the field, and they are beautiful. Certainly He will also _____ _____.

Psalm 100:2—As a child of the LORD I serve Him with _____ and come before Him with _____ _____.

VI. Complete one of the following projects.

1. Write a prayer you could say after recovering from sickness.

2. Write a hymn verse in which you thank God for His gifts to you.

3. Make a poster in which you remind people that God preserves His people from evil.

4. Write a poem in which you remind people of gifts from God that are often taken for granted.

UNIT 19 The Second Article—Redemption
Jesus Christ, Both God and Man

"God so loved the world that He gave His one and only Son." (John 3:16)

I. Draw a line through the words that are not true.

1. All that we are and hope to be we owe to (*our parents—ourselves—Jesus*).
2. *Jesus* means (*holy—Savior—Messiah—divine*).
3. *Christ* means (*The Anointed One—Savior—Caesar*).
4. *Messiah* means (*king—The Anointed One—Savior*).
5. Jesus Christ is (*greater than—equal to*) God the Father.
6. Jesus Christ is (*both God and man—only God—only man—one third of God*).

II. Write a G before the statements that show Jesus to be true God and an M before those statements that show Him to be true man.

1. _____ At the baptism of Jesus the Father said, "This is My beloved Son."
2. _____ Jesus told His disciples, "Look at My hands and My feet."
3. _____ Jesus said, "All power is given to Me."
4. _____ Jesus quieted a storm.
5. _____ Jesus was born in Bethlehem and laid in a manger.
6. _____ Jesus knew 40 years before it happened that Jerusalem would be destroyed.
7. _____ Jesus wept at the grave of Lazarus.
8. _____ Jesus became thirsty as He hung on the cross.
9. _____ Jesus raised the daughter of Jairus from the dead.
10. _____ Angels sang at Jesus' birth.
11. _____ Jesus died and was buried.
12. _____ Jesus rose from the dead and ascended to heaven.

III. Number the following events in the order in which they took place. (Number one has been inserted for you.)

_____ God loved Adam and Eve and promised them a Savior.

_____ Jesus Christ, God's only-begotten Son, was born of an earthly mother at Bethlehem more than nineteen hundred years ago.

__1__ God made Adam and Eve holy.

_____ For thousands of years believers waited for the Savior to come.

_____ God would not permit sinful people to stay in Paradise.

_____ Adam and Eve sinned by disobeying God.

IV. Check (✓) those activities that may show thankfulness to Jesus for the salvation He has given.

1. _____ studying religion memory work diligently
2. _____ helping your father and mother
3. _____ cheating to get good grades in school
4. _____ being selfish
5. _____ attending church regularly
6. _____ using God's name needlessly
7. _____ helping people who are having a hard time
8. _____ being satisfied with what you have
9. _____ praying regularly

V. Write T before the true statements and F before the false statements.

1. _____ God hates sin.
2. _____ God hated people after the fall.
3. _____ God's love for people caused Him to promise a Savior.
4. _____ Jesus was true God before all time. He is eternal.
5. _____ Jesus was true man when Adam lived.
6. _____ Ever since His birth at Bethlehem, Jesus is true God and true man at the same time.
7. _____ Jesus was holy because Mary, His mother, was holy.
8. _____ Jesus proved Himself to be true God by doing mighty works called miracles.
9. _____ Jesus became a human being so that He could show us how to live and thus earn heaven for ourselves.

VI. Long before Christ was born, the Old Testament prophets spoke of His coming. Read these Bible passages, and write answers to the questions.

Isaiah 7:14—What would the Savior be called?

_____

Micah 5:2—In what town would the Savior be born?

_____

Isaiah 11:1—Who is the Branch that would grow in Jesse's family?

_____

Deuteronomy 18:15—Who is the Prophet whom the Lord would raise up?

_____

Isaiah 9:6—What other names have been given to the Savior?

_____   _____

_____   _____

UNIT 20 The Second Article—
Redemption
The Suffering of the God-Man

"Look, the Lamb of God, who takes away the sin of the world!" (John 1:29)

I. Number the following in the order in which they happened in the life of Jesus.

_____ crucified   _____ born of the Virgin Mary
_____ poor, hated, persecuted   _____ suffered under Pontius Pilate
_____ buried   _____ died

II. Fill in the spaces with the correct words from the Word Box.

Word Box

love
punishment
sins
God's
holy
save
righteous
all
clean
willingly

1. Jesus __ __ __ __ __ __ __ __ __ suffered His painful
   death because of His __ __ __ __ for all people.

2. Jesus took upon Himself our __ __ __ __ and suffered
   our __ __ __ __ __ __ __ __ __ __.

3. Jesus shed His holy blood to make us __ __ __ __ and
   __ __ __ __ __ __ __ __ __ before God.

4. Jesus' blood can make the foulest person __ __ __ __ __
   because it is the blood of __ __ __' __ own Son.

5. Jesus suffered and died in order to __ __ __ __ us.

6. Jesus is the Savior of __ __ __ people.

III. From your *Living in Christ* text write the Bible verse citation that could be used to help a person who made each of the following statements understand the truth about Jesus.

1. Christ died only for the believers. _____

2. Jesus could not help dying; so many people were against Him.

   _____

3. Jesus was punished for His sins. _____

4. We can get rid of our sins by doing good things for others.

   _____

5. A rich man can buy his way into heaven by giving a large amount of money to the
   church. _____

IV. Write in the missing words from this hymn; see *LW* 98:1.

Glory be to ___ ___ ___ ___ ___,

Who in ___ ___ ___ ___ ___ ___ pains

Poured for me the ___ ___ ___ ___ ___ ___ ___ ___ ___

From ___ ___ ___ sacred veins.

V. Underline the ending that makes each sentence a true statement.

1. *Redeem* means (*sass—love—buy back*).
2. Jesus redeemed us with His (*love—blood—gold*).
3. Jesus came to earth to (*save us—heal the sick—show us how to live—preach*).
4. *Purchased* means (*bought—suffered—crucified*).
5. *Precious* means (*holy—innocent—of high value*).
6. *Condemned* means (*sinful—guilty—sentenced to punishment*).

VI. Jesus' great suffering and death took place during Holy Week. Number the following events in the order in which they happened. (Number one has been inserted for you.)

_____ betrayed by Judas in Gethsemane

_____ died on the cross

_____ sweat drops of blood

_____ condemned by Caiaphas and the elders

__1__ instituted the Lord's Supper

_____ found innocent by Pilate

_____ prayed in Gethsemane

_____ scourged and mocked by Pilate's soldiers

_____ buried

_____ condemned by Pilate

_____ crucified

VII. Read and meditate on the hymn "Jesus, I Will Ponder Now" (*LW* 109). Answer the following questions as you meditate and then complete the last activity.

1. Why does the hymn writer ask that he be endowed with the Holy Spirit? _____

   _____

2. Describe the deep affliction that Jesus suffered. _____

   _____

3. For whom did Jesus suffer deep affliction? _____

   _____

4. If my sins give me alarm, what is the cure? _____

   _____

5. Write a prayer to conclude your meditation on this hymn. _____

   _____

   _____

UNIT *21* The Second Article—Redemption
The Redeeming Death of Jesus

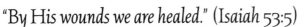

"By His wounds we are healed." (Isaiah 53:5)

I. According to Luther's explanation of the Second Article, from what three evils has Christ purchased and won us? List the three evils below.

1. _____
2. _____
3. _____

II. Each of the following stories from the life of Christ shows His power over one of the three great evils from which He has redeemed us. Write the letter of the evil before the title of the story in which Jesus is shown to have power over that evil.

A. Sin

B. Death

C. Devil

1. _____ The Temptation of Jesus, Matthew 4:1–11

2. _____ The Man Who Was Paralyzed, Matthew 9:1–8

3. _____ The Young Man of Nain, Luke 7:11–15

4. _____ Zacchaeus, Luke 19:1–10

5. _____ The Woman of Canaan, Matthew 15:21–28

6. _____ The Resurrection of Christ, Mark 16:1–8

III. Each of the following situations shows how Christ has saved us from sin, death, or the devil. Write *sin*, *death*, and/or *devil* before each sentence to indicate which of the three is conquered.

1. _____ Isaac was very sick, but he was not afraid to die.

2. _____ Anthony was tempted to steal fruit from the store, but he left the store without taking anything.

3. _____ Lee Anne sleeps soundly after she has asked Jesus to forgive the wrongs she did during the day.

4. _____ When Susan is tempted to say bad things about another girl, she is helped to not make her comments by remembering that Jesus loved His enemies.

5. _____ Keshawn's grandmother died. He knows he will see her again in heaven.

6. _____ Unbelieving people in one country stopped sacrificing animals when the Gospel of Jesus' redeeming love was preached to them.

IV. Underline the names of those who serve their Savior with thankful hearts for all He has done for them.

1. Marjie often fails to attend church.

2. Kelsey invited his friend to go to church with him.

3. Harry is a real problem to his parents; they worry about him because he disobeys them, his teachers, his coaches, and others who try to help him.

4. Emily has a habit of lying to her teacher.

5. Cliff says his morning and evening prayers thoughtfully.

6. Franci is kind to others; she especially tries to be kind to people who tease her.

7. Philip quarrels with someone almost every day.

8. Stephanie prepares her schoolwork carefully.

V. Describe two ways in which you can show that you belong to Christ, who redeemed you from sin, death, and the devil.

_____

_____

_____

_____

_____

_____

_____

_____

UNIT 22 The Second Article— Redemption
The Resurrection and Ascension of Jesus

"Thanks Be to God! He gives us the victory through our Lord Jesus Christ."
(1 Corinthians 15:57)

I. To make true statements about Jesus, our Savior, join the sentence endings in Group Two to the beginnings in Group One. Write the letter of the correct ending for each sentence on the line at the end of the sentence.

GROUP ONE	GROUP TWO
1. Our Savior died and was buried, but _____	A. we shall live also.
2. Jesus descended into hell in order to _____	B. show that He was the victor over sin and Satan.
3. By His resurrection from the dead, Jesus showed that _____	C. He rose from the dead on the third day.
4. Because Jesus lives, _____	D. rule over the world for the good of those who believe in Him.
5. Our Lord ascended into heaven to _____	E. He is truly the Son of God and the Savior of the world.

II. Underline all endings to these statements that state biblical teachings.

1. Jesus descended into hell *(because hell is the devil's home—to save us from hell—to show Himself as the victor over sin and the devil—to finish suffering for our sins).*

2. Jesus ascended into heaven *(40—6—12)* days after His resurrection.

3. After His resurrection Jesus showed Himself to the disciples and many other friends to convince them that *(He is the Son of God—He was no longer dead—God was satisfied with His suffering—all believers shall rise from death to live forever).*

4. Jesus ascended into heaven to *(prepare an eternal home for believers—leave us —suffer for us—rule the world for the good of believers).*

5. "He sits at the right hand of God" means *(His chair is next to God—He has the full power of God to rule for the benefit of the church—He is between the Father and the Holy Spirit).*

III. Number the following events to indicate the order in which they happened.

_____ Jesus ascended into heaven.

_____ Jesus rose from the dead.

_____ Jesus sits on the right hand of God.

_____ Jesus descended into hell.

_____ Jesus showed Himself alive to His friends.

IV. Write T before the true statements and F before those that are false.

1. _____ Christ's body only seemed to be dead.

2. _____ Christ descended into hell to suffer some more.

3. _____ Christ's suffering ended when He died.

4. _____ By rising from the dead, Christ showed that He is true God.

5. _____ Only believers will rise from the dead on the Last Day.

6. _____ Jesus is still a true man, even after He ascended into heaven.

7. _____ If Christ had remained dead, you could still go to heaven.

8. _____ Now that Jesus has ascended into heaven, He no longer helps believers.

9. _____ The disciples were never really sure that Jesus was alive again.

10. _____ My Savior suffered, died, and rose from the dead for me; now I can be sure that I, too, shall live with Him eternally.

V. Write some words of advice or comfort that you could give to each of these people.

1. Shirley, at times, is afraid to go to sleep because she fears she may die in her sleep.

_____

2. Roberto doesn't think he should tell other people that Jesus died for them.

_____

3. Khalid's friend says that he will go to heaven if he just tries to lead a good life.

_____

4. Norma says that Pilate and the Jews were the only people responsible for Jesus' suffering.

_____

5. Lynn doesn't attend church very often, but she is certain she will be saved because she believes and was baptized.

_____

VI. After His resurrection Jesus appeared to people on several occasions. Compile a list of people who saw the risen Christ. Then create a poster with this or a similar title: We Know Christ Is Risen!

UNIT 23 The Second Article— Redemption
The Last Judgment

IXΘYC

"He will reign for ever and ever." (Revelation 11:15)

I. Study the Bible passages in *Living in Christ;* then write three different factual statements about Christ's second coming.

1. _____
_____

2. _____
_____

3. _____
_____

II. Write endings for these sentences that agree with what the Bible teaches.

1. The exact time for the coming Judgment Day is

_____

2. Jesus will come in glory to

_____

3. The Last Day will be a day of doom for

_____

4. Christians will be very happy on the Last Day because

_____

III. Read Matthew 24:1–28 and then check (✓) the events below that are signs of the Last Day.

1. _____ False prophets will try to fool believers.
2. _____ Wars and rumors of wars will happen.
3. _____ Airplanes will be developed.
4. _____ Famines will occur.
5. _____ Peace on earth will exist everywhere for 1,000 years.
6. _____ Earthquakes will take place.
7. _____ Contagious diseases will develop.
8. _____ Christians will be persecuted and hated.
9. _____ People will love each other less and less.

47

10. _____ Believers will rule the world.

11. _____ The Gospel will be preached to all nations.

12. _____ Great happiness will exist throughout the world for 1,000 years.

IV. Underline the names of those who look forward with faith in Christ to the coming of the Last Day.

1. Gary prays that he may always remain a believer.

2. Mary is certain that Judgment Day will not happen during her life.

3. Christine looks forward to seeing Jesus face-to-face.

4. Rakeen hopes Judgment Day will not come while he is young. He wants to enjoy having some fun first.

5. Matt dreads the thought that all the great things in the world will be burned up when Jesus comes.

6. Cary knows that she will be happy on that day because she loves and trusts in Jesus with all her heart.

V. Place a check mark (✓) before the descriptions of those people whom Jesus will place on His right hand on Judgment Day.

1. _____ A condemned murderer who confessed his faith in Jesus an hour before he was put to death.

2. _____ A woman who was baptized but didn't believe in Jesus for the rest of her life.

3. _____ An old man who was never baptized but, by the power of the Holy Spirit, became a believer shortly before he died.

4. _____ A believer who had been a great sinner.

5. _____ A person who went to a Christian church regularly, acted like a good Christian, helped many poor people, but didn't really trust in Jesus for forgiveness of sins.

6. _____ A believer who spent his life serving God and his neighbors.

VI. Check (✓) those activities that are good ways to prepare for seeing Jesus on the Last Day.

_____ 1. quarreling with others in your family

_____ 2. praying regularly for those who are sick

_____ 3. hating a person who picks on you

_____ 4. being jealous of someone who is a good athlete

_____ 5. asking God for a strong faith

_____ 6. helping the poor

_____ 7. saying mean things

_____ 8. forgiving your enemies

_____ 9. planting a tree

_____ 10. sassing parents and teachers

_____ 11. telling others of Jesus' love

_____ 12. asking the Holy Spirit to keep us in the faith until death

UNIT 24 The Third Article — Sanctification
The Holy Spirit

"I will pour out My Spirit on your offspring, and My blessing on your descendants." (Isaiah 44:3)

I. Write the words from the Word Box in the spaces below to state biblical teachings about the Holy Spirit and the Christian faith.

Word Box

helpless
invites
Christ
opens
change
sanctifies
gives
Holy Spirit
keeps
Savior
Gospel
faith

1. Without God I am __ __ __ __ __ __ __ __.
   I can understand nothing about __ __ __ __ __ __,
   our __ __ __ __ __ __.

2. Only the __ __ __ __ __ __ __ __ __ __ is able to
   work a __ __ __ __ __ __ in my heart.

3. The Holy Spirit __ __ __ __ __ __ __ me to come to
   Christ, __ __ __ __ __ me power to lead a godly life,
   and __ __ __ __ __ me in true __ __ __ __ __
   until I die.

4. After leading me to faith in Christ, the Holy
   Spirit __ __ __ __ __ __ __ __ __ __ me.

5. The Holy Spirit does this work by means of
   the __ __ __ __ __ __.

II. Number the parts of the following story in the order in which they happened. The first one has been done for you. Four of the parts tell about the workings of the Holy Spirit; write *called, enlightened, sanctified,* or *kept* to tell what the Holy Spirit did in each part of the story.

____ _____ With the Holy Spirit's help, I love my Savior and serve Him through godly living.

____ _____ Then, at a funeral, I heard a pastor speak of Christ's great love for me. He said Jesus suffered and died for my sins.

____ _____ When I am tempted to return to the way I used to live or to doubt Jesus' love, I am reminded of Christ's love when I hear words of forgiveness in church. I know that the Holy Spirit will keep me in the true faith throughout my life.

_1_   I was an unbeliever; I was interested only in having fun and living a comfortable life.

____ _____ I began to realize my sinful condition and knew that I would not be saved if Judgment Day came today. I asked Jesus to have mercy on me and forgive all my sins.

III. Underline the names of those children who give evidence that they have been sanctified by the Holy Spirit.

1. Les, by habit, uses God's name to curse and swear.

2. Bill is honest with everyone.

3. Gene loves to help his mother.

4. Lee likes to brag about his good behavior and his regular church attendance.

5. Glen will not go to a movie that has a lot of fighting.

6. Ellie never shares her candy with her friends.

7. Deedee gives part of her spending money to help missionaries.

IV. Write T before true statements and F before those that are false.

1. _____ The Holy Spirit is true God.

2. _____ The Holy Spirit is more holy than the Father.

3. _____ The Holy Spirit leads us to become Christians.

4. _____ To become a believer is impossible without the Holy Spirit.

5. _____ Unbelievers can do good works that are pleasing to God.

6. _____ The Holy Spirit makes people believe by appearing to them in dreams.

7. _____ The Holy Spirit works faith in a baby's heart through Baptism.

8. _____ It is the Holy Spirit's fault when people are unbelievers.

9. _____ I could not remain a believer if it were not for the Holy Spirit.

10. _____ I can believe in Jesus Christ without the help of the Holy Spirit.

V. Read the Bible references and answer the questions.

1. Luke 11:13—Who gives the Holy Spirit to us?

_____

2. John 14:16–17—What are two other names given to the Holy Spirit?

_____   _____

3. John 16:13—Who will guide us into all truth?

_____

4. 1 Corinthians 6:11—What three things has the Holy Spirit done for believers?

_____   _____

_____

5. John 14:26—In whose name does the Holy Spirit do these things?

_____

6. 1 Corinthians 3:16—Who lives in your heart?

_____

UNIT 25   The Third Article —
Sanctification
The Holy Christian Church, the Communion of Saints

"Christ loved the church and gave Himself up for her." (Ephesians 5:25)

I. Review the Bible Teachings section and then write the endings for these sentences.

   1. Believers in Christ are brothers and sisters in the

      — — — — — — — — — — — — —.

   2. We call this family the

      — — — — — — — — — — — — — — — — — — — — — —.

   3. The Christian church is *holy* because the believers are cleansed of all their sins

      by the ___ ___ ___ ___ ___ ___ ___ ___ ___ ___ ___ ___ ___.

   4. ___ ___ ___ ___ ___ ___ is the only foundation of the church.

   5. All members of the holy Christian church are one body, of which

      Christ is ___ ___ ___ ___ ___ ___ ___.

   6. Only God knows who the true members of the church are, because ___ ___

      — — — — — — — — — — — — — — — — — — —

      the ___ ___ ___ ___ ___ ___ ___ ___ of ___ ___ ___ ___ ___ ___ ___ ___ ___

      — — — — — — — — — — or not ___ ___ ___ ___

      — — — — — — — —.

   7. Every believer is a member of the ___ ___ ___ ___

      — — — — — — — — — — — — — — — — — ___, or the

      — — — — — — — — — — — — — — — — — — — — —.

II. From Luther's explanation of the Third Article, list five things that the Holy Spirit does for the holy Christian church.

   1. _____

   2. _____

   3. _____

   4. _____

   5. _____

III. Write the term from the Word Box that each phrase describes. Some terms may be used more than once; some will not be used.

Word Box

Lutheran church

Jesus Christ

Holy Spirit

faith

holy Christian church

believers

my church

Peter

1. the rock on which the church is built _____

2. all believers in Christ, both living and dead _____

3. temples of the living God _____

4. people in whom the Holy Spirit lives _____

5. the spiritual body of which Christ is the head _____

6. the foundation of the holy Christian church _____

7. something we cannot see in our neighbor's heart _____

8. the large family to which people of all religious denominations belong when they trust in Jesus as their Savior from sin

_____

9. the building in which I worship on Sunday _____

10. the body of which I always want to be a member

_____

IV. To become and to remain members of the holy Christian church should be our highest aim. Test yourself in this important matter by placing a check mark (✔) in the column that you think best describes your Christian life. Then write a prayer for the Holy Spirit's blessing on your Christian life.

	Usually	Sometimes	Never
1. I say morning and evening prayers.			
2. I regularly ask Jesus for forgiveness.			
3. I actively participate in family devotions.			
4. I forgive those who sin against me.			
5. I give gladly to support my church.			
6. I am eager to learn God's Word.			
7. I think of my Baptism to remind me that I am God's child.			

V. These Bible passages will tell you whether the statements are true or false. Read the passages and circle either the T for true or F for false after each statement.

1. 1 Peter 4:16	I should be happy to suffer for Christ.	T	F
2. Acts 20:28	Christ purchased the church with His blood.	T	F
3. Ephesians 5:25	Christ loved the church and gave Himself for it.	T	F
4. Colossians 1:18	The church has no head.	T	F
5. Romans 8:9	In order to belong to Christ, we must have His Spirit.	T	F

UNIT 26  The Third Article — Sanctification
The Forgiveness of Sins

"The Lord is full of compassion and mercy." (James 5:11)

I. Match the sentence endings on the right with the beginnings on the left by writing the letters on the lines.

1. The members of God's family are happy because _____

2. Even believers, who love Jesus, _____

3. To remain God's children, _____

4. Christ earned the forgiveness that we _____

5. We say we are saved by grace because, _____

A. people need forgiveness each day.

B. although we do not deserve it, God forgives us for Jesus' sake.

C. sin every day.

D. they trust that their sins are forgiven through Jesus.

E. receive as a free gift from God.

II. In each sentence underline all the endings that make true sentences.

1. God assures us of the forgiveness of our sins (*every Sunday—only once a day—every Good Friday—through His Word*).

2. Jesus won forgiveness for (*the Christian church—all people—unbelievers*).

3. Forgiveness is *offered* to (*repentant believers—all who hear the Gospel—church members*).

4. Forgiveness is *received* by (*repentant believers—all people—those who trust their good works*).

5. To receive forgiveness, we need to (*attend church—keep the commandments—repent of our sin—trust that Jesus is our Savior*).

6. Forgiveness is something we (*earn—receive by God's grace—deserve*).

7. No one receives forgiveness unless he or she is (*confirmed—honest—sorry for his or her sins—a believer in God's promise of forgiveness through Jesus*).

8. Forgiveness is received from (*God—the pastor—the church*).

III. When God forgives sins, He expects us to amend our sinful lives and sin no more. How might these people amend their lives in thankfulness to our forgiving God?

1. Martha will not go to church when the weather is unpleasant. _____

_____

2. Gil uses curse words on the playground. _____

_____

3. Josey promises to do what her mother asks her to do, but then she forgets to do it.

_____

4. Carol kept back part of her church offering to attend the circus. _____

_____

5. Wayne will not admit he did wrong because he is afraid he will be punished.

_____

6. Mary picks on her little brother. _____

_____

7. Kewaan goes to movies that have many sexually explicit or violent scenes. _____

_____

8. Laurie takes money from her mother's purse without telling her. _____

_____

9. Charlie doesn't complete his religion homework. _____

_____

IV. Match each Bible passage with the truth it teaches about the forgiveness of sins by placing the numbers on the lines in front of the appropriate passage.

_____ Romans 3:23   1. Repentance and remission of sins should be preached to people of all nations.

_____ Matthew 9:6

                         2. For Jesus' sake God forgives even the evil thoughts that are in all our hearts.

_____ Luke 23:34
                         3. Everybody has sinned.

_____ Luke 24:47
                         4. Jesus has the power to forgive sins.

_____ Acts 8:22
                         5. The Lord is good and always ready to forgive.

_____ 1 John 1:9
                         6. Jesus asked His Father to forgive those who crucified Him.

_____ Psalm 86:5   7. If we confess our sins, God will forgive us.

V. Complete one of the following projects.

1. Design a weekly prayer book; include a page for each day of the week. Write a prayer for each day. Allow room for prayers to be added. Make an appropriate cover for your book.
2. Write a prayer in which you ask for forgiveness.
3. List all places in the Communion service (*Lutheran Worship*, pp. 178–196) in which worshipers ask for forgiveness.

UNIT 27 The Third Article —
Sanctification
The Resurrection of the Body and the Life Everlasting

"In My Father's house are many rooms." (John 14:2)

I. Using the words in the Word Box, write in the missing words to complete this paragraph about the end times. Some terms will be used more than once.

Word Box

> heaven
> death
> grave
> sin
> live
> soul
> Christ
> faith
> glory
> raise
> body
> pain
> joy
> God
> Judgment

When I die, my __ __ __ __ will leave my body, but it will not die. Since I have believed in __ __ __ __ __ __, when my eyes are closed in death, my soul will at once go to __ __ __ __ __ __ __. My __ __ __ __ will be laid to rest in a __ __ __ __ __ and will return to the dust from which it was made.

On __ __ __ __ __ __ __ __ Day God will __ __ __ __ __ my body and take it to __ __ __ __ __ __, where it will again be united with my __ __ __ __. My glorified body will be perfect, free from __ __ __, __ __ __ __, and __ __ __ __ __. In heaven I will __ __ __ __ in unending __ __ __ and __ __ __ __ __ with Jesus.

I pray to __ __ __ that He will keep me in the one true __ __ __ __ __ forever.

II. Match these Bible stories with the truths they teach by writing the numbers on the lines. Sometimes more than one number may be used.

1. The Ascension of Jesus
2. Elijah's Ascension
3. The Young Man of Nain
4. The Rich Man and Poor Lazarus
5. The Good Samaritan
6. The Daughter of Jairus
7. Stephen
8. The Raising of Lazarus

_____ God has power to raise the dead.

_____ For Christians death is like a sleep.

_____ Believers would rather die than deny their Savior.

_____ Jesus returned to heaven to prepare an eternal home for believers.

_____ Faith shows itself in good works.

_____ God has taken some people to heaven while they were still alive.

_____ God can raise dead bodies that have decayed.

_____ Angels carry the believer's soul to heaven.

III. While it is true that only faith in Jesus saves, Christians must not forget that good works are the fruit of faith. God expects us to show our faith by a God-pleasing life (Matthew 25:31–46). Underline the names of those Christian children who are exhibiting the fruits of their faith.

1. John could not attend school for five weeks because of a broken leg. Neal visited him after school several times a week and helped him with his homework.

2. The children collected money to buy John a prayer book. Dameon received five dollars from his mother to help buy the gift, but he spent it for ice cream.

3. Kevin's outgrown clothes are still in good condition. He asked his pastor for the name of a family that might be able to use them.

4. Julie treated the new girl in the neighborhood so kindly that her family later enrolled her in the Lutheran school that Julie attended.

5. Helen often uses part of her allowance to go to the show, but she never contributes to the offerings at church.

6. Eunice and Glenn persuaded a group of children to go with them to sing carols for the shut-ins at Christmas time.

7. Anya often helps a neighbor lady with her housework.

8. Colin likes to bully the younger children into doing what he wants them to do.

9. Oshane doesn't know Kip very well, but he defends Kip when other kids say mean things about him.

10. Sue never shares her snacks with a girl in her class who can't afford any.

11. Paul knows that his pastor and his teacher are very busy. He likes to help them when he can at church and school.

IV. Look up each Bible reference and then write a statement summarizing what the reference teaches about the Judgment Day.

1. 1 Thessalonians 4:16_____

_____

2. 1 Thessalonians 4:17_____

3. John 14:2 _____

4. Daniel 12:2 _____

_____

5. 1 Corinthians 6:9 _____

_____

6. Revelation 14:13 _____

_____

UNIT 28 The Introduction

"Lord, teach us to pray." (Luke 11:1)

I. Use the words in the Word Box to complete the sentences. The Bible Teachings section of *Living in Christ* will help you.

Word Box

lips
people
teaches
everywhere
times
will
prayer
enemies
Lord's Prayer
Jesus
talk
freely
better
father
every

1. God wants His children to speak ___ ___ ___ ___ ___ ___ with Him, just as most children are not afraid to speak to their own ___ ___ ___ ___ ___ ___.

2. A heart-to-heart ___ ___ ___ ___ with God is known as ___ ___ ___ ___ ___ ___.

3. It is not a prayer if we speak with our ___ ___ ___ ___ only.

4. God wants us to pray for all ___ ___ ___ ___ ___ ___ on earth, even for our ___ ___ ___ ___ ___ ___ ___.

5. God wants us to pray ___ ___ ___ ___ ___ ___ ___ ___ ___ ___ and at all ___ ___ ___ ___ ___.

6. God hears ___ ___ ___ ___ ___ prayer that is spoken in the name of ___ ___ ___ ___ ___ and is according to His ___ ___ ___ ___.

7. God, at times, gives us something ___ ___ ___ ___ ___ ___ than what we had requested.

8. Jesus taught His disciples the ___ ___ ___ ___' ___ ___ ___ ___ ___ ___ ___.
   In it He ___ ___ ___ ___ ___ ___ ___ us how to pray.

II. Write a sentence to explain what is wrong in each of these statements.

1. Nearly all my prayers should be addressed to God. _____

_____

2. God hears most of my prayers. _____

_____

3. I can get along without praying. _____

_____

4. I should only pray for myself and for my friends. _____

_____

5. Saints in heaven hear and answer some of my prayers. _____

_____

6. God gets tired of listening if I pray too often. _____

_____

7. I have a right to tell God *when* He should answer my prayer. _____

_____

8. A believer's prayer is no better than an unbeliever's prayer. _____

_____

9. The only good place to pray is in church. _____

_____

10. Grown people don't need to say bedtime prayers. _____

_____

III. Most hymns are prayers addressed to God. "Now the Day Is Over" (*LW* 491) is an example of such a prayer. Think about this prayer as you answer the questions below.

1. What do we ask Jesus to give each of these groups of people in this prayer?

the weary _____

those who suffer _____

those who plan evil _____

children falling asleep _____

2. What three things do we ask for ourselves?

_____

_____

3. Why is stanza 6 a good way to end a prayer?

_____

_____

IV. Consult the hymnal *Lutheran Worship* to answer the following questions.

1. What are the most often used closing words of each of the 55 prayers included in *Lutheran Worship*, pages 124–133?

_____

2. Why is this a good ending for so many prayers?

_____

UNIT 29 The First Three Petitions
Praying for Spiritual Blessings

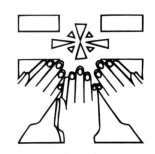

"Seek first His kingdom and His righteousness." (Matthew 6:33)

I. In the *Small Catechism* Martin Luther organized his study of the Lord's Prayer into an introduction, seven petitions, and a conclusion. The seven petitions can be grouped under three headings. Write the words of the Lord's Prayer that belong in each section.

I. Introduction

_____

II. Three petitions for the welfare of our own and our neighbor's soul

_____

_____

_____

III. One petition for bodily blessings

_____

IV. Three petitions for deliverance from evils

_____

_____

_____

V. Conclusion

_____

_____

II. Write the numbers 1, 2, or 3 before each of the following short prayers to indicate whether it is related to the First, Second, or Third Petition.

_____ Help us to do Your will.

_____ Lord, help us keep Your name holy.

_____ Make us eager to tell others about Your Son, Jesus, our Savior.

_____ Help us to lead a godly life.

_____ Keep me in the Christian faith until I die.

_____ Keep me in Your kingdom.

_____ Send Your Holy Spirit to enlighten me more in the knowledge of Your Son.

_____ Protect me from the evil will of the devil, the world, and my sinful heart.

_____ Protect me from false teachings; keep Your pure Word in my heart.

III. The sentences below state various truths about praying. Each statement is taught in a Bible passage. Match the Bible reference with the truth it teaches by writing the appropriate letter on the line in front of each statement.

A. Matthew 21:22

B. Matthew 5:44

C. 1 Timothy 2:8

D. Psalm 50:15

E. John 16:23

_____ When you are in trouble, pray; God will help you.

_____ Jesus promises that when we believe, we will receive what we ask in prayer.

_____ God wants us to pray for everyone, even for our enemies.

_____ You may pray anywhere.

_____ God the Father will give us the things we pray for in Jesus' name.

IV. Complete the following checklists. Discuss them with your classmates and family.

1. In this list check (✓) those activities that are ways to hallow God's name.

_____ Memorize Bible passages.

_____ Take notes to help yourself concentrate on a sermon.

_____ Laugh when you hear a curse word.

_____ Read the Bible each day.

_____ Cheat if you have to in order to win a game.

_____ Respect your parents.

_____ Hate someone who hates you.

_____ Give to the needy.

2. In this list check (✓) those activities that let God's kingdom come.

_____ Be truly repentant.

_____ Invite a friend to church.

_____ Finish a spelling assignment during your religion lesson.

_____ Pray for a strong faith.

_____ Never make contributions to support your church.

_____ Tell playmates of our Savior's love for them.

3. In this list check (✓) ways to do God's will on earth.

_____ Hang out with kids who like to steal from stores.

_____ Complain when your parents refuse to buy the expensive sports shoes you want.

_____ Pray for help to think pure thoughts.

_____ Treat your friends as you want them to treat you.

_____ Don't object when you hear children use God's name in vain.

_____ When you are tempted to sin, say, "Get away from me, Satan."

_____ Ask God for Christian friends.

UNIT 30 The Fourth Petition
Praying for Daily Bread

"You open Your hand and satisfy the desires of every living thing." (Psalm 145:16)

I. Write T or F to tell whether these sentences are true or false.

1. _____ God gives daily bread both to believers and to unbelievers.

2. _____ The Fourth Petition deals only with food.

3. _____ Daily bread is a gift that I may demand of God.

4. _____ People who are too lazy to work deserve to be fed.

5. _____ My purpose in life should be to become rich.

6. _____ "Take no thought for tomorrow" means "do not plan for the future."

7. _____ Everything I have in life is a gift from God.

8. _____ Sharing my earthly blessings with those who need help pleases God.

9. _____ God feeds only those people who pray to Him.

10. _____ I displease God when I worry about the future.

11. _____ God wants me to pray that all people receive daily bread.

12. _____ Once a year, on Thanksgiving Day, I should thank God for His blessings.

II. Describe what you would do in each of these situations.

1. Your teammates call and ask you to come out to play ball. You have finished eating, but the others at the table have not finished and your family has not said the prayer of thanks.

    _____

2. Your seat in a restaurant is at a place where many people could watch you pray.

    _____

3. You arrive for supper after the family has already prayed. _____

    _____

4. You are at home alone and are about to eat the meal you prepared. _____

    _____

5. After several months of unemployment your father finally finds work. _____

    _____

6. You read in the paper that throughout your country there have been bumper crops.

    _____

7. Your church has suggested that the members give an offering to help a family whose home recently burned.

_____

8. Your father's salary is low. You earn money by delivering newspapers. What would you do with your income?

_____

9. On your birthday you remember that during the past year you were never sick.

_____

III. Read each Bible reference and then identify the bodily blessing God gave in each instance.

Matthew 14:13–21 _____

John 2:1–11 _____

1 Kings 17:1–16 _____

Exodus 16:4–15 _____

Luke 5:1–9 _____

IV. Complete the projects list below.

A. In *Lutheran Worship* (pp. 124–133) many special prayers are provided. Some of them ask for daily bread blessings. List several of the blessings requested in these prayers.

_____

B. List five particular blessings in addition to food and drink for which you are thankful.

1. _____   2. _____

3. _____   4. _____

5. _____

C. Write a short paragraph describing how a Christian might celebrate Thanksgiving Day.

_____

_____

_____

_____

UNIT *31* The Last Three Petitions and the Conclusion
Praying for Deliverance

"The LORD will watch over your coming and going." (Psalm 121:8)

I. Write 5, 6, or 7 to show which petition fits each of these short prayers.

_____ Keep us from giving in to temptations that come to us.

_____ Forgive our sins for Jesus' sake.

_____ Keep every evil away from us.

_____ Give us willing hearts to think and act kindly toward those who sin against us.

_____ Do not stop listening to our prayers even though we are sinful.

_____ When our time comes to leave this world, Lord, take us into Your heavenly kingdom.

_____ Preserve us from falling into unbelief and from participating in shameful activities, both things that the devil wants us to do.

_____ Lord, if You will not remove the burden from my back, strengthen my back to bear the burden.

II. Underline the names of those people who appear to ask for forgiveness in the right spirit when they say the Lord's Prayer.

1. For two weeks Josey would not talk with the girl who told on her.
2. Dylan plans to play a mean Halloween trick on the neighbor who scolded him for running across his yard.
3. Jean isn't angry with the friend who accidentally broke her doll.
4. After saying the Lord's Prayer, Joshua decided not to tell his teacher the lie that would have saved him from being punished.
5. Hailey tries to be kind to the neighbor girls who laugh at her for going to Sunday school.
6. Samantha doesn't talk to girls she doesn't like.
7. Iesha forgave the girl who lied about her.

III. God will help us overcome temptation to sin. With God's help, what might you do to overcome each of these temptations?

1. missing church _____

2. looking at unclean pictures in magazines _____

3. cursing, [misusing] God's name _____

4. fighting with other children _____

5. lying _____

6. grumbling when your parents ask you to do something

_____

IV. When people give in to temptation, it is their own fault, not God's. Draw a line through the actions that may lead people to give in to temptation; then circle those actions that help people resist temptation.

1. choosing companions who take drugs
2. reading books about fortune-telling
3. watching and praying
4. idling away time
5. working hard to get rich
6. studying to get the best grades in your class
7. working honorably each day
8. remembering Jesus' suffering for you
9. not caring about God's Word
10. hearing and trusting God's Word

V. Read these Bible passages and answer the questions.

Jonah 1:15–17; 2:1–10—From what evil did God deliver Jonah?

_____

Job 5:19—When trouble comes to you, what will God do?

_____

Psalm 91:11—What is one way that God protects you from evil?

_____

Hebrews 12:6—Why does the Lord at times allow troubles to come to us?

_____

John 17:15—What did Jesus ask His Father to do for those who believe?

_____

VI. Complete the following activities.

1. After reading Luther's explanation of the Seventh Petition, write the four areas of our lives in which we may suffer evil.

   a. _____ b. _____

   c. _____ d. _____

2. Think of one evil that could happen to you in each area mentioned above.

   a. _____ b. _____

   c. _____ d. _____

3. Why does God allow sorrow and suffering to enter a believer's life? _____

   _____

4. What does the word *amen* mean?

   _____

UNIT 32 The Nature of Baptism

"Repent and be baptized, every one of you, in the name of Jesus."
(Acts 2:38)

I. Match the sentence endings with their beginnings by writing the letters on the blank lines.

1. When I was baptized I became _____

2. My Baptism delivered me from death and the devil by _____

3. Christ commanded His church to baptize _____

4. A tiny baby _____

5. After a child has been baptized, the sponsors will _____

A. a child of God.

B. pray for him/her and help him/her to learn God's Word.

C. everyone, regardless of age or race.

D. washing away my sins.

E. can be saved through Baptism.

II. Fill in these items if you have been baptized. Copy the information from your baptismal certificate.

I was baptized by Pastor _____ on

_____, when I was _____ old.

My sponsors were

_____   _____

_____   _____.

III. Use the words in the Word Box to fill in the missing words.

Word Box

water
Baptist
pastor
Christian
faith
Christ
children
words
John

1. The command to baptize was given by ___ ___ ___ ___ ___ ___.

2. The man who baptized Jesus was ___ ___ ___ ___ the ___ ___ ___ ___ ___ ___ ___.

3. The words "all nations" means the ___ ___ ___ ___ ___ ___ ___ ___ too.

4. Whenever possible the ___ ___ ___ ___ ___ ___ of a church should perform the Baptism.

5. If a child is very sick and there is no time to call a pastor, any ___ ___ ___ ___ ___ ___ ___ ___ ___ may baptize.

6. If a baptized person permanently loses his ___ ___ ___ ___ ___, he will not be saved.

7. It is a proper Baptism only if we use ___ ___ ___ ___ ___ and the ___ ___ ___ ___ ___ that Jesus commanded us to use.

IV. *Lutheran Worship* page 312 has a form for Holy Baptism in Cases of Emergency. What are the two features necessary for a proper Baptism?

    1. _____

    2. _____

V. From Luther's answer to the question *What is Baptism?* write two reasons why Baptism is not simple water only.

    1. _____

    2. _____

VI. Look up these passages in your Bible and identify the people who were baptized.

    Matthew 3:5–6 _____

    Matthew 3:13–17 _____

    Acts 19:1–5 _____

    Acts 2:41 _____

    Acts 8:26–38 _____

    Acts 9:17–18 _____

    Acts 16:14–15 _____

VII. Answer each question in a sentence or two.

1. Why do Christian parents have their children baptized as soon as possible?

_____

_____

2. Why do Christian parents have their children baptized as infants if at all possible?

_____

_____

3. Why are some people lost even though they have been baptized?

_____

_____

4. What are some of the benefits of having baptismal sponsors for children?

_____

_____

5. Why does the congregation present the baptized person with a baptismal certificate?

_____

_____

UNIT 33 The Benefits of Baptism

"[Christ cleansed the church] by the washing with water through the Word." (Ephesians 5:26)

I. Baptism is a means of grace through which God gives us the blessings that Christ has won for us. Name three blessings Luther mentions in his answer to the question *What benefits does Baptism give?*

1. _____

2. _____

3. _____

These blessings are given to all who __ __ __ __ __ __ __ this.

II. Use the words in the Word Box to write in the missing words. Some words are used several times.

Word Box

water
washing
Holy
God
faith
rebirth
Spirit
Word
renewal
Baptism

When I was baptized, it was not only the __ __ __ __ __ that brought the great blessings, but the __ __ __ __ of __ __ __ that the pastor spoke. Without the __ __ __ __ of God, applying the __ __ __ __ __ only is not a __ __ __ __ __ __ __.

If through __ __ __ __ __ I trust the __ __ __ __ of God combined with the water, the Baptism is a __ __ __ __ __ __ __ of __ __ __ __ __ __ __ and __ __ __ __ __ __ __ by the __ __ __ __ __ __ __ __ __ __.

III. Check (√) the attitudes and activities that are signs of the new life the Holy Spirit has worked in us through Baptism.

_____ quarreling
_____ jealousy
_____ faith in Jesus as our Savior
_____ desire to use resources wisely
_____ hatred
_____ bragging
_____ a forgiving heart
_____ speaking kind words

_____ using filthy speech
_____ thinking pure thoughts
_____ love for money
_____ copying music from the Internet illegally
_____ love for Christ
_____ humbleness
_____ repenting of sins

_____ attending church regularly

_____ eagerness to study God's Word

_____ giving money to support mission work

_____ cheating on schoolwork

_____ praying for others

_____ sharing with the needy

IV. Correct these sentences by rewriting them.

1. I refuse to be baptized, but I can still get to heaven.

_____

_____

2. All baptized people go to heaven.

_____

_____

3. Anyone who is not baptized will be damned.

_____

_____

V. Number the following items to show the order in which they usually follow one another. The first one has been numbered for you.

_____ God-pleasing life

_____ faith and forgiveness

_____ Baptism

_____ death

_____ everlasting life

__1__ birth

_____ lack of faith

VI. Read each Bible passage; then match it with the truth it teaches about Baptism by placing the letter on the line in front of the passage.

_____ 1 Peter 3:21

_____ Mark 1:4

_____ Ephesians 4:5

_____ Acts 2:38

_____ Acts 22:16

A. John baptized for the remission of sins.

B. Baptism gives us the gift of the Holy Spirit.

C. Baptism saves us.

D. Baptism washes away sins.

E. We have one Lord, one faith, and one Baptism.

UNIT 34 The Authority to Forgive Sins

"Repent and believe the good news." (Mark 1:15)

**I. Fill in the missing words in these sentences. Use the Bible Teachings section in
Living in Christ as a guide.**

1. We publicly confess our sins before God and ask forgiveness in almost

   __ __ __ __ __   __ __ __ __ __ __ __   __ __ __ __ __ __ __ __ __.

2. The pastor forgives our sins in the __ __ __ __   __ __   __ __ __.

3. All __ __ __ __ __ __ __ __ __ have God-given power to

   __ __ __ __ __ __ __ __ __   __ __ __ __ __.

4. Public forgiveness is given by the __ __ __ __ __ __, who has been

   __ __ __ __ __ __ for this purpose.

5. Forgiveness should be given only to repentant believers who are truly

   __ __ __ __ __ for their sins.

6. The power to __ __ __ __ __ __ __ sins is called the Office of the

   __ __ __ __.

7. Heaven is closed to people who do not have forgiveness of __ __ __ __ through Jesus.

**II. Use the Bible Readings section of *Living in Christ* to obtain help with this
exercise. Write the Bible verse that teaches the truths listed below.**

1. All people must admit that they are sinners. _____

2. Called pastors forgive sins in the name of Christ. _____

3. God will forgive any believer who confesses his or her sin. _____

4. The power to forgive and to retain sins was given to all the disciples. _____

5. Forgiveness of sins is the key that unlocks the gates of heaven. _____

**III. Match each term with its meaning by writing the number of the meaning on the
line before the term.**

_____ remit sin

_____ absolution

_____ penitent

_____ retain sin

_____ confess sin

1. forgiveness given by a called pastor or fellow Christian
   to a penitent sinner
2. hold a person to be still guilty of sins
3. forgive
4. admit guilt for sin
5. sorry for sin and believing in Jesus as the Savior

69

IV. Place an X before the correct ending for each sentence.

1. The pastor forgives sins because

    ___ a. they are done intentionally.

    ___ b. God has given him power to do so in His name.

2. Any believer can

    ___ a. forgive sins done against him or her.

    ___ b. lock heaven by refusing to forgive.

3. Sins should be forgiven only to believers who

    ___ a. go to church.

    ___ b. confess and are sorry.

    ___ c. lead good lives.

4. By refusing to confess sins we

    ___ a. harm our good reputation.

    ___ b. lock our gateway to heaven.

5. Before God we should confess

    ___ a. most of our sins.

    ___ b. all sins.

    ___ c. those sins we know.

V. Explain what is sinful in each of these examples. Write what each person should have done.

1. The boys played a mean trick on Barke. He said, "I'll never forgive you as long as I live."

    _____

    _____

2. In church and school Carolyn says prayers asking for forgiveness, but she never really feels sorry for her sin.

    _____

    _____

3. Chimelu made fun of Xolani, who had been caught stealing.

    _____

    _____

4. Jerry was stubborn and would not admit that he had lied to his mother.

    _____

    _____

5. Rita felt bad that she had kicked her brother when she was angry, but she never asked to be forgiven.

    _____

    _____

VI. Complete one of the following special exercises.

1. On a sheet of paper write a prayer asking God to forgive a sin you have done. Following your prayer write the words from *Lutheran Worship*, page 158, that your pastor speaks when he absolves (forgives) sinners in church.

2. Make a poster that features the words *I forgive you for Jesus' sake.*

UNIT 35 The Nature of the Sacrament

"This is My body. . . . This is My blood." (Mark 14:22–24)

I. Match the sentence endings to their beginnings by writing the letters of the endings on the blank lines.

1. The Sacrament of the Altar is also called _____

2. We receive Christ's true body and blood _____

3. We cannot understand how Christ can give His _____

4. We believe that we receive Christ's true body and blood because _____

5. Jesus wants us to _____

6. Christ Himself instituted the Holy Supper _____

7. In this Sacrament Christ gives His true body and blood to us Christians _____

A. body and blood with the bread and wine.

B. to eat and to drink.

C. in the Holy Supper.

D. receive the Sacrament often.

E. the Lord's Supper.

F. on Maundy Thursday evening.

G. God's Word says, "This is My body" and "This is My blood."

II. Tell how each of these statements conflicts with what Scripture teaches.

1. People who receive the Lord's Supper only imagine that the body and blood of Christ are received with the bread and wine in Holy Communion.

_____

2. We do not receive bread and wine in Holy Communion because they have been changed into Christ's body and blood.

_____

_____

3. Believers can celebrate Holy Communion without bread and wine.

_____

4. Going to the Holy Supper is only a fine custom.

_____

5. The body and blood of Christ are holy; therefore the bread and wine should be adored.

_____

III. Write T or F before these sentences to show whether they are true or false.

1. _____ Bread, wine, body, and blood are all present in the Lord's Supper.

2. _____ The disciples were the first people to receive the Lord's Supper.

3. _____ The power of this Sacrament lies in the bread and wine.

4. _____ Jesus said that we should imagine that we receive His body and blood in the Sacrament.

5. _____ It is not necessary for communicants to drink the wine because they already receive some of Christ's blood together with His body in the bread.

6. _____ "This do in remembrance of Me" means that believers should go to the Sacrament and be reminded of their Savior's suffering, death, and resurrection.

7. _____ We should go to the Sacrament at least twice, but not more than four times, a year.

8. _____ Another name for the Lord's Supper is *The Holy Eucharist*.

IV. Using *Lutheran Worship* (pp. 170–174) arrange these portions of the Communion Liturgy in the correct order by numbering them. The first one has been numbered for you. Circle the two that you think are the most important.

_____ The Pax Domini (The Peace)   _____ The Benediction

_____ The Sanctus (Holy, Holy, Holy)   _____ The Words of Institution

_1_ The Preface   _____ The Post Communion Canticle

_____ The Thanksgiving Prayer   or Nunc Dimittis

_____ The Distribution   _____ The Agnus Dei

_____ The Lord's Prayer

V. Circle the names of those children who show respect for the Sacrament even though they are not old enough to commune.

1. Ernie doesn't care to attend church on Communion Sunday because he says the service is too long.

2. Jon sings the hymns as his own prayers while the people are receiving the Sacrament.

3. Russ thinks children shouldn't be expected to sit through the Distribution because it is really for grown-ups.

4. Roberto prayed that his older brother, who doesn't receive the Lord's Supper regularly, would change his ways.

5. Dewaan and Hal whispered and giggled continually during the Distribution.

VI. Study the stanzas of *Lutheran Worship* 249. Summarize the teaching about the Lord's Supper taught in the following stanzas.

1. Stanza 3 _____

_____

_____

2. Stanza 4 _____

_____

UNIT 36 The Benefits of the Lord's Supper

"Whoever comes to Me I will never drive away." (John 6:37)

I. In answering the question *What is the benefit of this eating and drinking?* Luther mentions three precious gifts that are given to those who receive the Sacrament. List them.

1. _____

2. _____

3. _____

II. Luther says the power of the Lord's Supper is not in the bodily eating and drinking, but it is in the words *given and shed for you for the forgiveness of sins*. Explain what he means by this statement.

_____

_____

_____.

III. To be truly worthy and well prepared for receiving the benefits of the Lord's Supper, one must have _____ in the words

_____

_____.

IV. Using the Bible Readings section of *Living in Christ*, write the biblical reference for a passage that teaches each of these truths.

1. Jesus wants *all* sinners to seek forgiveness from Him. _____

2. Jesus gave His body and blood for the forgiveness of our sins. _____

3. Before partaking of the Lord's Supper, we must make certain that we really trust His words. _____

4. If an unbeliever goes to the Lord's Supper, he or she receives no forgiveness of sins.

_____

5. By God's grace all people have available to them salvation through the blood of Jesus.

_____

V. Write a word from the Word Box in each sentence to make a true statement.

Word Box

- faith
- soul
- examine
- children
- forgiveness of sins
- still more sure

1. The Lord's Supper is food for the ___ ___ ___ ___.
2. Christ offers ___ ___ ___ ___ ___ ___ ___ ___ ___ ___ ___ ___ ___ ___ ___ ___ to all who eat and drink of His body and blood.
3. Before going to the Sacrament, we must ___ ___ ___ ___ ___ ___ ___ ourselves to make certain we have ___ ___ ___ ___ ___ in Christ's promise.
4. When we receive His body and blood, the Holy Spirit makes us ___ ___ ___ ___ ___ ___ ___ ___ ___ ___ ___ ___ of forgiveness.
5. The Lord's Supper should not be given to little ___ ___ ___ ___ ___ ___ ___ ___ or others who have not been prepared for Communion.

VI. Answer each of the following questions.

1. Why is no sin too great to be forgiven?

_____

_____

2. A believer receives forgiveness daily by asking Jesus for forgiveness with a repentant heart. Why, then, is it necessary for believers to receive the Sacrament?

_____

_____

3. Why is self-examination before communing so important?

_____

_____

VII. Complete one of the following projects.

1. Write a prayer for a friend or relative who does not receive Holy Communion often.
2. Read the Christian Questions with Their Answers in *Luther's Small Catechism with Explanation* (pp. 39–42). Then write a short essay explaining why these questions and answers "are no child's play," as Luther notes (p. 42).
3. Read the prayers for use Before Reception of Holy Communion, After Reception of Holy Communion, and For Right Reception of Holy Communion in *Lutheran Worship* (p. 128). Then write a devotion for your own use based on one of these prayers. Share your devotion with your family or class.

Life of Christ Crossword Puzzle

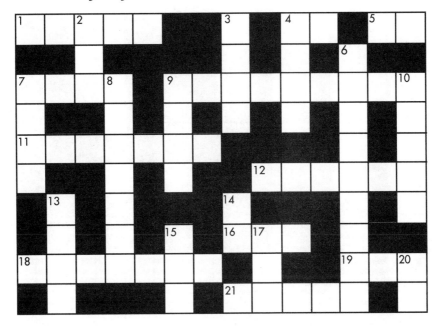

Across

1. Matthew 1:21—She will give birth to a Son, and you are to give Him the name _____.

4. John 3:16—For God _____ loved the world that He gave His one and only Son.

5. Mark 15:34—"_____ God, _____ God, why have You forsaken Me?"

7. Matthew 1:21—He will save His people from their _____ .

9. Romans 4:25—He was _____ over to death for our sins.

11. Romans 6:23—The gift of God is _____ life in Christ Jesus our Lord.

12. Matthew 16:16—You are the _____, the Son of the living God.

16. Matthew 9:6—The Son of _____ has authority on earth to forgive sins.

18. Born of the Virgin Mary, suffered under _____ Pilate, was crucified, died, and was buried.

19. Matthew 10:22—He who stands firm to the _____ will be saved.

21. 1 John 1:7—The _____ of Jesus, His Son, purifies us from all sin.

Down

2. Matthew 3:17—This is My _____, whom I love.

3. Matthew 27:34—They offered Jesus wine to drink, mixed with _____.

4. Luke 19:10—For the Son of Man came to seek and to _____ what was lost.

6. Matthew 27:35—When they had _____ Him, they divided up His clothes by casting lots.

7. Colossians 1:20—Through Him to reconcile to Himself all things . . . by making peace through His blood, _____ on the cross.

8. Philippians 2:7—But made Himself nothing, taking the very nature of a _____.

9. John 19:33—But when they came to Jesus and found that He was already _____, they did not break His legs.

10. Matthew 6:12—Forgive us our _____ , as we also have forgiven our debtors.

13. 2 Corinthians 8:9—Though He was rich, yet for your sakes He became _____.

14. John 18:5—"I _____ He," Jesus said.

15. 1 Peter 2:24—He himself bore _____ sins in His body on the tree.

17. Galatians 3:26—You are _____ sons of God through faith in Christ Jesus.

20. Luke 23:34—"Father, forgive them, for they _____ not know what they are doing."

Martin Luther Crossword Puzzle

Across

1. To help children learn Christian doctrine, Luther wrote the Small _____.

4. He refused to recant his writings at _____ in 1521.

5. Luther promised this saint that he would become a monk if she rescued him.

7. Luther taught that there is _____ only through Jesus.

10. Luther contributed much to the _____ of the church.

12. This family introduced Luther to culture, music, and the arts.

13. Luther discovered in the Bible that he could never do enough good works to please _____.

14. Luther taught at this university.

Down

1. Luther helped write the Augsburg _____.

2. In the Ninety-five _____ Luther protested against the sale of indulgences.

3. Luther married Katherina von _____.

6. The town where Luther was born and died.

8. Luther first attended school here.

9. While a "prisoner" at the _____ Castle, he translated the New Testament into German.

11. Luther earned his Master's Degree at the University of _____.